From the Chief Executive

The Queen's Diamond Jubilee

On behalf of the employees of Royal Mail Group, I would like to offer my sincere congratulations to Her Majesty Queen Elizabeth II on her Diamond Jubilee.

More so than any other British business, Royal Mail Group has a deep and enduring tie to the monarch. The image of Her Majesty Queen Elizabeth II is recognisable throughout the world as the symbol of United Kingdom postage.

Throughout the first 60 years of her reign, it has been our tremendous good fortune that Royal Mail products have such a strong and close affinity with Her Majesty. In our two Diamond Jubilee stamp issues, we celebrate the role Queen Elizabeth II has played in the life of her Nation and Commonwealth.

We hope they will be seen as a fitting tribute to a remarkable Queen.

Moya Greene
Chief Executive Officer
Royal Mail Group

Royal Mail Group Ltd is registered in England and Wales. Registered number 4138203. Registered office: 100 Victoria Embankment, LONDON, EC4Y 0HQ

monarch
The Monarch Group

The Monarch Group is proud to participate in the celebration of the Diamond Jubilee of Her Majesty Queen Elizabeth II

Monarch, which comprises a number of the UK's longest established and best loved travel companies including Monarch Airlines, Cosmos Holidays and Monarch Aircraft Engineering has been one of the pioneers of the British travel industry.

Monarch is the only UK travel group bearing the same name and in the same ownership as it was when it was founded in the early years of Her Majesty's reign – a testament to the commitment of its founding shareholders, and its management and employees, many of whom have served the Group for years numbering in decades.

From its beginnings in the early 1960's, the Group has operated for over 50 years, remaining committed throughout to providing outstanding service and value to the travelling British public.

Its brands are well regarded for their integrity, heritage and customer offering in the leisure travel industry in the UK and across Europe.

The Monarch Group wishes to join others in taking the opportunity to show its sincere appreciation in these pages to Her Majesty Queen Elizabeth II on the occasion of her Diamond Jubilee, and to express our gratitude for this long and continuing period of unwavering commitment.

1960'S

1961 and 1967
Cosmos Tours and Airline Engineering Limited launched

1970'S

Monarch Aircraft Engineering Limited enters jet aircraft maintenance and Monarch Airlines becomes an all jet fleet. Expansion for Cosmos Tours offering increased UK departure points

1980'S

Expansion for Monarch Aircraft Engineering into new UK airports, whilst Monarch Airlines carries one million passengers annually, is the first charter airline worldwide to order Boeing 757 next generation aircraft and launches scheduled flights, Monarch Crown Service

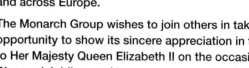

1968
Talks established between the companies to provide aircraft capacity to Europe. Monarch Airlines launched with two Bristol Britannia 312 aircraft and Airline Engineering Limited renamed as Monarch Aircraft Engineering Ltd

1990'S

Monarch Airlines takes delivery of two Airbus A330 aircraft bringing two-class seating to the long haul charter market. Further expansion for Monarch Aircraft Engineering Ltd and Cosmos acquires seat only operator, Avro

2000'S

Monarch Airlines expands its scheduled flight network to include two further UK bases. Monarch Aircraft Engineering expands into Europe and Cosmos launches accommodation-only brand, somewhere2stay and offers real-time flexible duration holidays

2011/12

- Monarch Airlines offers capacity for 7 million passengers and strengthens scheduled services
- Cosmos celebrates its 50th anniversary
- Monarch Aircraft Engineering ranked 9th largest MRO in Europe, North Africa and the Middle East

Contents

I vividly remember that moment at Eton in February 1952 when the chapel bell began its sad toll indicating some dire event and then noticed, from the window of my room at Jourdelay's, the Royal Standard at half mast on the flagpole of the Round Tower at Windsor Castle. Silently and slightly confused we congregated in Chapel to be told the news that the King had died.

Since that moment we have been very fortunate to enjoy sixty years with Her Majesty, Queen Elizabeth II as our Head of State and let us all now show our gratitude and appreciation for her leadership and devotion to duty which has had such a marked effect upon the fortunes and happiness of us all.

Long live the Queen. Long may she reign.

The Earl Cadogan, DL

Cadogan
18 Cadogan Gardens
London SW3 2RP

In this exciting and celebratory year for Her Majesty the Queen, Shell staff join together in sending our heartfelt congratulations to Her Majesty for 60 successful years on the throne.

Over the past six decades, our country, like the rest of the world, has changed enormously; the Queen has led our country through these changes, not only with wisdom and dignity, but also with a deep understanding of how important it is to adapt and evolve to meet the challenges of modern day life.

We are extremely proud to be citizens of the United Kingdom and of the wider Commonwealth, and we gratefully acknowledge the role that Her Majesty has played in maintaining the United Kingdom's reputation around the world. We wish her a very happy Diamond Jubilee.

Managing Editor
Laura White

TRBL Adviser
Afsheen Latif

Art Director
Paula Lock

Head of Publishing Operations
Andy Roberts

Production Controller
Sema Demir

Group CEOs
Dean Citroen & Oren Wolf

Group CFO
James Ward

Financial Controller
Scott Griffin

Sales Director
Warren Hayward

Sub Editor
Isobel Clark

Writers
Content Kings

Published by
CW Publishing Group
3rd Floor, 3 Upper Street
London N1 0PH
Tel: +44 (0)33 3344 1350
Web: www.cwcomms.com

Printed in Spain by
Rivadeneyra, S.A.
Tel: +34 91 208 91 50

Colour origination by
F1 Colour
Tel: 020 7620 0644

Paper supplied by
Denmaur Papers Plc
Tel: 01795 426775

Cover Images
Getty Images

Welcome

Thank you for purchasing our Official Souvenir Guide for the Queen's Diamond Jubilee.

It is with the greatest pleasure that I, as national president of The Royal British Legion, welcome you to join with us in celebrating the Diamond Jubilee of our patron, Her Majesty Queen Elizabeth II. Read here about the essential work that the Legion performs for serving and ex-Service personnel and their dependants, as well as the life and successes of Elizabeth II, her relationship with her twelve prime ministers, and the impressive military careers of the royals, right up to and including the young princes William and Harry.

Building the profile of The Royal British Legion is helped in no small part by the support of Her Majesty the Queen. What the Queen has done for this country is amazing, not just because monarchy itself is such an important unifying factor and something which is truly great about the UK, but also because, she, herself, is such a wonderful individual.

As a nation, it is clear to see that we are so proud of her – people throughout the world hold our Queen in the highest regard and have tremendous admiration for her, which is a source of great pride for the country. Long may she reign.

John Kiszely

Sir John Kiszely
National President of The Royal British Legion

Standard Chartered

Celebrating Her Majesty The Queen's Diamond Jubilee

Standard Chartered congratulates Her Majesty the Queen on the 60th year of her reign.

Here for good
standardchartered.com

🇬🇧 UNITED KINGDOM

In 2012, Her Majesty the Queen will become the second monarch in British history to celebrate 60 years on the throne.

The Queen's achievements – her hard work and dedication across this extraordinary time – are a cause for great celebration by us all, both in this country and across the wider Commonwealth.

As patron of The Royal British Legion since 1952, the Queen has played an important role in shaping its values and ensuring that it remains at the forefront of the charitable support that is provided to our Armed Forces.

Her Majesty's close relationship with the Armed Forces, past and present, is also epitomised through the role that she has played for the last 60 years in leading the National Service of Commemoration at the Cenotaph, which recognises and remembers all those who have lost their lives fighting for their country.

I am delighted that the Legion have decided to produce this commemorative brochure, and that charitable causes will benefit from its sale. I wish the project every success.

David Cameron

David Cameron
Prime Minister

**At Aviva, we're not about policies, we're about people.
So I'd like to salute a truly exceptional one.**

Her Majesty the Queen.

Over the past sixty years, our monarch has built up a reputation for wisdom and integrity and for being a much loved, trusted and respected ambassador for Great Britain. It's a reputation that none of us could hope to emulate but, it's something that at Aviva, we aspire to.

From the moment Her Majesty ascended to the throne, she took her responsibilities to people around the world to heart and carried them out with grace, intelligence and a very human touch. If you start as you mean to go on, set high standards and continue to uphold them, you're more likely to attain long-term, sustainable success.

I personally cannot think of a finer example of this than Her Majesty's long and glorious reign. Her first duty has always been to her people and at Aviva, our first duty has always been to ours; that's why 44 million people around the world put their trust in us. For over 300 years, in good times and bad, we've recognised that they need to feel secure and our role is to provide that sense of security.

We're here to help secure their prosperity and peace of mind and it's a huge responsibility. We protect almost every aspect of our customers' lives: their families, their health, their possessions, their whole futures. Over the years, we've looked after some very famous customers - Sir Isaac Newton, Sir Winston Churchill and John F Kennedy are a few of the better known ones. Yet we treat them all to the same high levels of service, always acting in their best interests, whoever they are and wherever they live. When I say "we", I mean the people who work for Aviva and we are proud to do so. Every day my colleagues will suggest new ways in which we can improve our business and the services we offer and this is something I really value.

At Aviva we believe we have to keep evolving because that's exactly what the world does. You only have to look back over the past sixty years to see how much it's changed but one thing has stayed constant and secure – the reign of Her Majesty Queen Elizabeth II.

So we feel privileged to be given the chance in this commemorative publication, to offer Her Majesty our warmest congratulations on her Diamond Jubilee.

Lord Sharman of Redlynch OBE
Chairman

AVIVA

NORWAY

It is an honour and a pleasure to extend to Her Majesty Queen Elizabeth II our warmest congratulations on the occasion of her Diamond Jubilee. Throughout her long reign Queen Elizabeth has served the British people with unfailing distinction, dignity and devotion. As monarch and head of state, she has inspired respect and admiration not only in Britain but all over the world. Hers has indeed been a lifetime of exceptional service. As neighbours and friends, Norwegians are pleased and proud to join in the Diamond Jubilee celebrations in recognition of the achievements during the past 60 years of a truly remarkable sovereign.

Long may she reign!

Kim Traavik

Ambassador of Norway to the United Kingdom

TURKEY

I would like to extend my congratulations on the occasion of the 60th anniversary of Her Majesty Queen Elizabeth II's accession to the throne of the United Kingdom. Having had the two concurrent grand empires in history and as two modern democratic states today at the opposite edges of Europe, Turkey and the United Kingdom have a long concerted history, an entrenched state experience, shared values and a common vision for the future. Today, Turkey and the United Kingdom enjoy a 'strategic partnership' based on historic and strong bonds of friendship and alliance. Our relations were fortified with historic visits. The first ever state visit by Sultan Abdülaziz to Britain in 1867 was celebrated as one of the most splendid and memorable events of its time. We were honoured with Her Majesty the Queen's state visits to Turkey; first in 1971 and then in 2008. Her Majesty Queen Elizabeth II extended generous hospitality to our President H E Mr Abdullah Gül during his state visit to the United Kingdom on 22-24 November 2011.

Having reigned for 60 years, Her Majesty's presence has served not only the British nation, but also the world. I am extending my best wishes for the well-being and prosperity of the friendly people of the United Kingdom, as well as Her Majesty the Queen's personal health and happiness.

Ünal Çeviköz

Ambassador of The Republic of Turkey to the United Kingdom

KENYA

On behalf of the Government and people of Kenya, I wish to take this opportunity to send our heartfelt and utmost congratulations to Her Majesty the Queen, on the auspicious occasion of her Diamond Jubilee.

The People of Kenya deeply appreciate the existing close ties and collaboration with the United Kingdom. We also appreciate Her Majesty the Queen's stewardship as the Head of the Commonwealth; the institution that has played a very central role in unifying all the 54 Commonwealth members. We acknowledge with gratitude the way that Her Majesty has steered the Commonwealth, keeping in touch with the developments through regular meetings with heads of governments, which have greatly reinforced the network of members.

As a member of the Commonwealth fraternity, Kenya continues to be active and subscribe to its fundamental principles of democracy, good governance, the rule of law and maintenance of international and stability in the world. We attribute the accrued social, political and economic benefits to the members of the Commonwealth and to the focused leadership provided by Her Majesty. Commonwealth stands out as a unique organisation amongst others international institutions.

Once again, on behalf of the Government and the people of Kenya, we are pleased to join the other distinguished foreign countries in congratulating Her Majesty the Queen on her successful 60 years on the throne.

Ephraim Ngare
High Commissioner
Kenya High Commission

The Life and Times

of Her Majesty, Queen Elizabeth II

A reflection on some of the most memorable events since the Queen's Coronation in 1953 to the present day

On 21 April 1926, a future Queen was born. Christened Elizabeth Alexandra Mary, her parents, Prince Albert and Elizabeth Bowes-Lyon, would both soon become British monarchs. Yet, in her early years, Elizabeth II was not expected to become Queen as she was third in the line of succession. This allowed her to have an upbringing free from the pressure and scrutiny that accompanies an heir apparent. Home-schooled at the Palace, Elizabeth met her future husband, Philip Mountbatten, at the Royal Naval College in 1939 and the pair fell instantly in love. They married in 1947 when Great Britain was still recovering from World War II. Due to the necessity of the times, Elizabeth had to collect clothing ration coupons to purchase the fabric for her wedding dress. The birth of Charles and Anne, in 1948 and 1950 respectively, followed soon after their marriage. After the death of her father

George VI in 1952, Elizabeth assumed the position as the ruling British monarch, where she has remained for nearly 60 years. In honour of her Diamond Jubilee year, we take a look at Queen Elizabeth II's extraordinary reign.

The Coronation

Although Elizabeth assumed the responsibilities of a ruling monarch in 1952, it wasn't until the following year that she received her Coronation. The ceremony, held on 2 June in Westminster Abbey, was the first of its kind to be televised. It is estimated that around 20 million Britons watched the ceremony on the BBC, with many buying their first ever TV set especially for the occasion. To ensure Canadians could view the event on the same day, footage was flown in to be aired by the Canadian Broadcasting Corporation. On her Coronation day, the Queen alluded to the rich history and tradition she had inherited: "I have behind me not   >>

Getty Images

"My Coronation is a declaration of our hopes for the future and for the years I may reign and serve you as your Queen"

Queen Elizabeth II and Prince Philip, Duke of Edinburgh, pass the Pool of Reflection at the Australian War Memorial in Canberra, 1954

only the splendid traditions and the annals of more than a thousand years but the living strength and majesty of the Commonwealth and Empire," she said. But Her Majesty urged her public to look onward to the future rather than back on the past, stressing that the Royal Family would not be an outdated archaism, but an important, relevant feature of 20th-century Britain. "My Coronation is not the symbol of a power and a splendour that are gone, but a declaration of our hopes for the future, and for the years I may, by God's grace and mercy, be given to reign and serve you as your Queen," she declared.

One of the most pressing duties for the newly crowned Queen was to oversee and manage the British Empire's transition towards a Commonwealth of Nations. Between 1954 and 1955 the Queen and Prince Philip, Duke of Edinburgh embarked on a momentous six-month tour of the Commonwealth nations. During the tour, they visited Bermuda, Jamaica, Panama, Fiji, Tonga, New Zealand, Australia, Cocos Islands, Ceylon, Aden, Uganda, Libya, Malta

and Gibraltar, travelling a total distance of 43,618 miles. In visiting New Zealand and Australia, Queen Elizabeth II became the first reigning Monarch of the two nations to pay an official visit to their shores. The Australian leg of the tour saw massive crowds flock to catch a glimpse of the Queen. Amazingly, over two-thirds of the population are estimated to have come out to see her.

The early years of her reign also saw the implementation of weekly meetings with the Prime Minister, a practice that continues to this day. The first of her weekly meetings was with Winston Churchill who heralded the beginning of a 'new Elizabethan age'. The Queen has attended every opening of Parliament except those in 1959 and 1963. Over the years, a number of prime ministers have remarked on her impressive political nous.

As the UK's head of state, HM Elizabeth II, has undertaken countless state visits to foreign countries, including a groundbreaking trip to Germany in 1965 (becoming the first British Monarch to visit the country since WWI). >>

Getty Images

On Christmas Day 1957, Queen Elizabeth II made her first live televised Christmas speech on the BBC. Twenty-five years previously, her father, George VI had made the first Christmas radio broadcast. The Queen's annual televised address has, in the subsequent 55 years, become as much a feature of Christmas Day as turkey, stuffing and Brussels sprouts!

The Queen further added to her air miles in 1957 with an historic state visit to the US to address the United Nations General Assembly. This was followed by a trip north to Canada to open the 23rd Canadian parliament (becoming the first Monarch of Canada to do so). In her youth Elizabeth learned French from a number of French and Belgian governesses. This linguistic proficiency has surprised and delighted French-Canadians on her visits to Francophone areas of Canada. The Queen's French fluency also allows her to converse freely with French-speaking ambassadors and heads of state. In her 60-year reign the Queen has undertaken an incredible 261 official overseas visits, including 96 state visits, to 116 different countries.

Children and grandchildren

In 1961, Elizabeth gave birth to her second son Andrew, later to become Duke of York. That same year, she toured Cyprus, India, Pakistan, Iran and Ghana. Though some felt the Queen's safety might be compromised while touring abroad, she dismissed those fears, not wanting to receive over-the-top security. Harold Macmillan wrote of the tour that: "The Queen has been absolutely determined all through (...) she is impatient of the attitude towards her to treat her as (...) a film star (...) She has indeed the heart and stomach of a man (...) She loves her duty and means to be a Queen."

In 1963, Elizabeth gave birth to her fourth and final child, Prince Edward. In July 1999, Edward married Sophie Rhys-Jones at Windsor Castle. Prior to the wedding ceremony Prince Edward was bestowed with the title of Earl of Wessex while Sophie became Countess of Wessex.

Queen Elizabeth II's reign coincided with many former British colonies, particularly those in Africa and the Caribbean, becoming independent nations. The '60s and '70s saw the most intense decolonisation with over 20 countries, including Cyprus, Jamaica, Nigeria and Sierra Leone, transitioning to self-governance. The United

Kingdom has been transformed utterly over the last 60 years but the Queen has remained a reassuring symbol of stability and national unity for Britons in an ever-changing political and geographical landscape.

In 1977, Elizabeth became a grandmother for the first time with the birth of Princess Anne's son, Peter Phillips,

"In 1977, Elizabeth became a grandmother for the first time with the birth of Princess Anne's son, Peter Phillips"

followed by Zara Phillips and then Prince Charles' son Prince William in June 1982. Today, Queen Elizabeth II has eight grandchildren: William, Harry, Peter, Zara, Beatrice, Eugenie, Louise and James. Peter and Autumn Phillips also gave the Queen her first great grandchild, Savannah.

The year 1977 was also significant because it marked Elizabeth's 25th year as Queen. On 7 June, over one million people lined the streets of London to celebrate the Silver Jubilee. The large crowds, many of whom had camped overnight, cheered excitedly as the Queen and Prince Philip led a procession to St Paul's Cathedral in the golden state coach.

St Paul's Cathedral was again the venue as Queen Elizabeth II's first child, Prince Charles, married Diana Spencer in July 1981. Billed as the wedding of the century, the ceremony was watched by an estimated 750 million people worldwide.

In April 1982, war broke out in the Falklands and the Queen had to watch on anxiously as Prince Andrew joined the crew of HMS Invincible as a helicopter pilot. Thankfully, Prince Andrew made it through the conflict unharmed and on the 23 July he married Sarah Ferguson at Westminster Abbey. Less than 90 minutes before the wedding service, the Queen conferred him with the title of Duke of York.

Remembering the Battle of Britain

In September 1990, The Queen participated in events marking the 50th anniversary of the Battle of Britain. A mass fly-past and a parade of RAF units and veterans were the main features of the commemorative occasion. >>

Clockwise from top left: Prince Charles and Lady Diana Spencer marry at St Paul's Cathedral, July, 1981. Prince Edward and Sophie Rhys-Jones marry at St George's Chapel, Windsor Castle, and become Earl and Countess of Wessex, 1999. The Queen plays with Princes Edward and Andrew at Windsor Castle, 1965

1952

CONGRATULATIONS TO
HER MAJESTY THE QUEEN
ON **60** GLORIOUS YEARS

2012

"In 1991 Queen Elizabeth II became the first ever British monarch to address a joint session of the US Congress"

In 1991 Queen Elizabeth II become the first ever British Monarch to address a joint session of the US Congress. During her speech, Her Majesty spoke of her belief that protecting the interests of a nation is better achieved through cooperation and compromise than force and coercion. "Some people believe that power grows from the barrel of a gun. So it can, but history shows that it never grows well, nor for very long. Force, in the end, is sterile. We have gone a better way: our societies rest on mutual agreement, on contract and on consensus," she said at the time.

Annus horribilis

The Queen is well known for her emotional restraint but she wore her heart on her sleeve when delivering a speech at Guildhall outlining just how difficult a year 1992 had been. At the beginning of the year, Prince Andrew and Sarah Duchess of York separated after four years of marriage. This was followed swiftly by the news that Prince Charles and Princess Diana's marriage was also coming to an end. To

add to this, two days before the Guildhall address, Windsor Castle suffered extensive fire damage. Luckily there were no serious casualties. To help pay for the costly renovations, the Queen decided to open Buckingham Palace to the paying public. During the heartfelt speech, Elizabeth famously described 1992 as her *annus horribilis*.

In 1997 tragedy struck with the death of Princess Diana in a Paris car crash. The Queen gave a speech the day before Diana's funeral expressing her admiration for the late Princess: "First, I want to pay tribute to Diana myself. She was an exceptional and gifted human being. In good times and bad, she never lost her capacity to smile and laugh, nor to inspire others with her warmth and kindness. I admired and respected her for her energy and commitment to others, and especially for her devotion to her two boys." The Queen further honoured Diana's life and charitable legacy by officially opening the Diana, Princess of Wales, National Memorial Fountain in 2004.

Whilst retaining the integral tradition and decorum expected of the Royal Family, the Queen has made   >>

Queen Elizabeth II addresses Congress in Washington, US, 1991

Getty Images

"A number of monuments and souvenirs were created to commemorate the Golden Jubilee, including a £5 coin"

great steps recently to make the monarchy more approachable and accessible. In particular, the Queen has shown a desire to keep the Royal Family relevant in the 21st century. In 1997, she oversaw the unveiling of the Royal website, www.royal.gov.uk; in 2006, Her Majesty's Christmas message was released as a podcast, and in 2007, she unveiled a YouTube Channel that would broadcast her annual address. In recent years, the Royal Family has also added Facebook, Flickr and Twitter accounts.

Golden Jubilee

On 6 February 2002, Elizabeth's 50-year anniversary as Queen was honoured. The Golden Jubilee was celebrated throughout the Commonwealth and beyond. A number of monuments and souvenirs were created to commemorate the momentous landmark, including a special £5 coin featuring an image of Elizabeth II mounted on a horse. Sadly, her Jubilee year also coincided with the news that the Queen Mother had passed away at the Royal Lodge at Windsor. During the Queen Mother's funeral ceremony in April, Westminster Abbey's tenor bell tolled once for each of her 101 years.

During her Golden Jubilee year, then-US President George W Bush made the first full state visit of a US President to the United Kingdom. Though this was the first official presidential state visit, during her reign the Queen has met,

From left: Queen Elizabeth II and the Duke of Edinburgh set out from Buckingham Palace in the Gold State Coach to St Paul's Cathedral, June 2002. Crowds gather outside for the Golden Jubilee celebrations, June, 2002

takes part in the spectacular Trooping the Colour parade. Trooping the Colour involves a military parade and march-past in which thousands of guardsmen parade the Colour (their regiment's flag).

Wedding anniversary

In November 2007 the Queen and Prince Philip celebrated their 60th wedding anniversary, becoming the first Royal couple to reach this marital landmark. Throughout their enduring relationship, Prince Phillip has been by Queen Elizabeth II's side, providing a constant source of comfort and support. The Queen summed up her feelings towards Phillip, stating: "He has, quite simply, been my strength and stay all these years, and I, and his whole family, and this and many other countries, owe him a debt greater than he would ever claim or we shall ever know."

In 2010, Elizabeth flew to New York to give the British Garden at Hanover Square its official Royal opening. The memorial in lower Manhattan remembers the 67 British victims of the September 11 attacks. There are plans to rename the memorial the Queen Elizabeth II Garden, to include victims from all Commonwealth countries killed in the attacks.

Last year saw the Queen make an historic state visit to Ireland at the invitation of the then-President of Ireland, Mary McAleese. The visit, the first by a British Monarch since George V in 1909, was an attempt to further improve relations between Britain and Ireland. During the Queen's visit, she attended a state dinner in her honour at Dublin Castle and laid a wreath in Irish National War Memorial Gardens. The Queen has always maintained the importance of honouring members of the Armed Forces who have lost their lives in battle. Every year on Remembrance

formally or informally, an incredible 10 US Commander-In-Chiefs. Queen Elizabeth II's most recent presidential meeting was with Barack Obama in 2009 at a state banquet in Buckingham Palace.

A proud day for Queen Elizabeth II was 12 April 2006 as her grandson, Prince Henry of Wales, or Prince Harry as he is more commonly known, graduated from the Royal Military Academy Sandhurst. The Queen, in her role as head of the Armed Forces, inspected the troops at the graduation ceremony. (Prince Harry is currently training to become an Apache helicopter pilot). Nine days after her grandson's graduation, the Queen celebrated her 80th birthday. Her Majesty marked the occasion with a walkabout in the streets outside Windsor Castle in front of throngs of well-wishers. The Queen celebrates two birthdays a year, her actual birthday on the 21 April and her official birthday on a Saturday in June. On her official birthday, Elizabeth

Getty Images

Looking after what people love in life since 1843

We are the UK's largest friendly society and its been 169 years since we welcomed our first customers when we started in 1843 as the 'Liverpool Independent Legal Victoria Burial Society' (later simply Liverpool Victoria). Our goal was to give financial security and peace of mind to more than just a privileged few. We started off as a burial society and for many decades we were most commonly associated with "penny policies" collected door to door by a countrywide team of agents, to provide a method of saving for people of modest means.

Of course, a lot has changed since we began but our core values remain the same. We still exist to offer products that will help people look after what they love in life so they can enjoy the peace of mind that comes with real financial security. Whether it's through insurance, investments or retirement solutions, we're committed to providing great value products and services and being easy to do business with.

We changed our brand to LV= back in 2007. The letters L and V retain our heritage as Liverpool Victoria and we inserted an equals sign as a modern-day expression of our mutuality.

Today, our values continue to underpin everything we do. As a mutual society, where one member has one vote, we're not answerable to shareholders. We channel all our energies and resources into doing what's right for you. That's why our products are regularly voted market leading and we win lots of awards.

defaqto 2011 ★★★★★ INCOME PROTECTION

defaqto 2011 ★★★★★ HOME INSURANCE

defaqto 2011 ★★★★★ CAR INSURANCE

RECOMMENDED PROVIDER which? www.which.co.uk Car Insurance July 2011

UK CUSTOMER EXPERIENCE AWARDS 2011 WINNER

WINNER £ Consumer Moneyfacts Awards 2011 Best Customer Service

Award winning

We've grown significantly over the past few years. We are now the UK's fourth largest car insurer and offer products such as travel, home, pet, income protection insurance and pensions.

Since 2007, and to support an expanding business we've created over 3,000 new jobs and have been voted one of the UK's top employers for the last four years. Our people have also contributed to our success in winning awards for great customer service.

LV=

Living our values

As part of living our values, we believe that we have a duty to help those less privileged than us and those that need support in our local communities.

The LV= Community Committees run by our own people decide which good causes and charities we should support and invest in – in and around the communities where they live and work.

One of our more major local initiatives is supporting LV= Streetwise – Dorset's award-winning interactive safety centre bringing safety awareness to children across the county.

Above left: HRH The Princess Royal visited the LV= Streetwise on 7th February 2008, unveiling a 10th anniversary plaque.

LV= SOS Kit Aid

As well as helping regional charities we also support national initiatives. One of these is as a sponsor of LV= SOS Kit Aid run by the Lords Taverners.

LV= SOS Kit Aid works by collecting donations of new and used kit from schools, sports clubs and manufacturers and passing it on to projects both in the UK and overseas. This year our support will mean that more than 20,000 young people who might not otherwise be able to take part in sports, will be given kit so they can join in. And by keeping the kit out of landfill sites, the scheme helps to promote a sustainable environment.

Sponsoring cricket

LV= SOS Kit Aid links into our sponsorship of cricket – the LV= County Championship. For over a decade we've supported the game at a grassroots level throughout the UK.

Left: HRH The Duke of Edinburgh with 2010 LV= County Championship winners Nottinghamshire

96% customer satisfaction across our product range

Over 5,000 employees

Five million customers

We pay out over £180m a year in savings and investment proceeds

A strong and independent mutual

We insure one in ten vehicles in the UK

Insurance 💙 Investments 💙 Retirement 💙   Visit LV.com

Prince William and Catherine Middleton marry in April 2011 at Westminster Abbey and become Duke and Duchess of Cambridge. The event was watched by an estimated two billion people globally

Sunday, the Queen, wearing all black, with the exception of red poppies, lays a wreath at the Cenotaph monument in Whitehall.

This summer, the Queen and the Duke of Edinburgh will lead the Opening Ceremony at the London Olympics and Elizabeth will launch the Paralympic Games for the first time.

This year is of course, the Queen's Diamond Jubilee year, with the main celebrations set to take place during an extended weekend from 2-5 June, of which the public have an extra Bank Holiday to enjoy the celebrations. Many communities are planning street parties and the Big Lunch idea suggests that neighbours dine together on the day. To honour the Queen's reign and her charitable legacy, Prime Minister David Cameron announced the creation of the Queen Elizabeth Diamond Jubilee Trust, which aims to "raise funds to invest in projects that will make a real and lasting impact on the lives of people".

Elizabeth spoke of her hope that the Jubilee year would serve as a reminder of the principles all Britons should aspire to. "In this special year, as I dedicate myself anew to your service, I hope we will all be reminded of the power of togetherness and the convening strength of family, friendship, and good neighbourliness, examples of which I have been fortunate to see throughout my reign and which my family and I look forward to seeing in many forms as we travel throughout the United Kingdom and the wider Commonwealth," Her Majesty said.

Wedding bells

Two of Queen Elizabeth II's grandchildren were married in 2011. Zara Phillips married English rugby player Mike Tindall in July at Canongate Kirk in Edinburgh. Earlier in the year, Prince William, second in line of succession, married Catherine Middleton in a grand ceremony at Westminster Abbey. Some estimates claim that close to two billion watched the event. Around 12 million Canadians tuned into the wedding, an incredible figure considering that the ceremony began at 6am Eastern Time and 3am Western Time. The Queen spoke of the two marriages in her Christmas address. "The importance of family has, of course, come home to Prince Philip and me personally this year with the marriages of two of our grandchildren, each in their own way a celebration of the God-given love that binds a family together."

Pastimes

Away from her duties as the British Head of State, the Queen likes to indulge in some of her favourite pastimes. She is famously an animal lover, taking a keen interest in horses. As an owner and breeder of thoroughbreds, she often attends race meets such as the Derby at Epsom and the Summer Race Meeting at Ascot. The Queen also >>

Congratulations to HM The Queen on her Diamond Jubilee.

United Utilities is the North West's water company. We keep the taps flowing and toilets flushing for seven million customers every day.

But behind the scenes, we run a 24-hour operation which is all about helping your life flow smoothly.

It's a hidden world of water pipes the length of motorways; sewers as high as buildings; space-age science labs and treatment works; and 5,000 employees stationed from Crewe to Carlisle. And a huge amount of pride, skill and technology goes into every drop of water that reaches your tap.

United Utilities

helping life flow smoothly

Proud to support the Royal British Legion's Diamond Jubilee 2012 souvenir guide.

For more information on what we do visit: **unitedutilities.com**

CELEBRATING A CROWNING ACHIEVEMENT.

The **Royal Canadian Mint** has a long history of honouring royal milestones through the stories behind our finely crafted collector coins.

We proudly join fellow Canadians in celebrating Her Majesty's Diamond Jubilee with these fine silver and ultra-high relief pure gold commemorative coins.

ROYAL CANADIAN MINT
MONNAIE ROYALE CANADIENNE

VISIT MINT.CA/DIAMONDJUBILEE

Getty Images

enjoys equestrian events. The Queen's horses have enjoyed success at major race meetings on a number of occasions. Famously in the 1956 Grand National Queen Elizabeth's horse Devon Loch, while in first place, inexplicably jumped into the air on the final stretch allowing the second placed horse to overtake. Queen Elizabeth took the incident well, memorably saying, "Oh, that's racing".

Sandringham, the Queen's country residence is home to a kennel of Labradors and cocker spaniels, which are used as gundogs. Corgis, however, are her breed of choice, and she is rarely seen without a litter of the small herding dogs at her ankles.

The Queen has a fondness for Scottish country dancing and often performs dances known as Gillies' Balls for staff and guests at Balmoral. Though quite reserved in public, many have credited Queen Elizabeth II with sharp wit and a good sense of humour. One story goes that at a garden party a young attendee's mobile rang as she was speaking with the Queen. As the mortified lady struggled to rush and silence the ringing, the Queen lightened the mood by saying, "You'd better answer that. It might be someone important!"

But spare time is rare for the Queen as she performs a huge amount of official and unofficial duties. She handles roughly 430 engagements each year and supports more than 600 charitable organisations and programmes. The Queen has conferred over 404,500 honours and awards, has sent almost 540,000 telegrams to couples celebrating their diamond wedding anniversary and over 175,000 birthday telegrams to centenarians. The Queen is undoubtedly the most widely travelled head of state in history and continues to span the globe well into her 80s.

Throughout her reign, the Queen has remained an emblem of national unity during times of disunity and has successfully managed the balancing act of retaining the Royal Family's institutions and traditions while ensuring that the monarchy remains relevant in the modern-day world. She is the second longest serving British monarch in history, recently overtaking George III's reign of 59 years and 96 days. Only her great, great-grandmother Queen Victoria, who reigned for 63 years, has enjoyed greater longevity. For these reasons her Diamond Jubilee year festivities will be enthusiastically celebrated throughout the UK, the Commonwealth and beyond. ∎

Queen Elizabeth II pats her horse, Balmoral Melody, at the Royal Windsor Horseshow on 11 May. The horse was named Supreme Champion of the Highland Pony class

Roll out the red carpet

Lord Harris would like to congratulate Her Royal Highness
on 60 years of magnificent reign

Born in 1942, Lord (Phil) Harris was just 10 years old when Queen Elizabeth came to the throne. Just five years later both his parents died of cancer in very quick succession, leaving Phil to take over his father's market stall and two linoleum shops, the kernel of the retailing empires he was to create over the next 50 years. Now Phil is one of Britain's most successful retailers, having established a formidable presence in the UK's flooring market, starting with Harris Queensway, then with Carpetright, Europe's leading specialist floor covering specialist with over 24% of the British flooring market, over 600 stores and employing over 2600 people in the UK, The Netherlands and Belgium.

'The key is to know what you want to achieve and then motivating people to achieve it', he says. 'You must also know what the customer wants, and the best way to do that is to talk to them'. For over 40 years, Harris has spent at least one day a week – usually Saturday – driving around his stores, chatting to the staff and customers, and sometimes even helping out by acting as a salesman himself, which he is supremely good at.

The success of Carpetright has enabled Phil to become a peer of the realm and a philanthropist. In his lifetime, Lord Harris and his family have generously given away nearly £150 million in charitable donations to a wide range of causes including £30 million to Guy's Hospital back in the 1970's when he spearheaded a brave attempt to turn the London hospital into the flagship of the Thatcher health service. There was also over £5 million to Great Ormond Street and £35 million for the Westminster Abbey Restoration Fund, a project very close to the heart of Prince

Philip, which Phil chaired for 10 years. But he takes most pride in his educational projects, including Harris Manchester College, Oxford and his own Harris Academy schools in South and East London. He created the first City academy 21 years ago when he took over a 'failed' school in Crystal Palace, which had a miserable 9% pass rate (measured as 5+ A* - C, including English and Maths). In 2011 the same school had a 95.5% pass rate, and is one of only three state schools in the country to be rated 'outstanding' in every department, with grades now exceeding many of the best-known public schools in the country. Last year more than 80% of its school leavers went on to University, three of them to Oxford. One girl got 6 A* grades.

There are now 14 Harris academies with 20,000 pupils, most of them from deprived backgrounds. Six of these schools have gone from 'failed' to 'outstanding' in two years, and overall grades across all the Harris schools are nearly three times the national average. The result is that the schools have been overwhelmed with applicants: 21,000 applications for 2,100 places in 2011. The Harris Academy, Beckenham attracted 1,500 applicants in 2011, against only 15 in its last year as the local authority-run school.

Harris pioneered the whole concept of the academy school, now adopted as the model which Michael Gove, the Education Secretary, and David Cameron have chosen to roll out across the country. Gove recently described Harris as 'one of the most admirable men I know' for his contribution to state education. The success of the schools in motivating both teachers and students was reflected by the fact that in the riots which tore London apart last year, not a single Harris student was reported to have been involved, despite the fact that many of the schools were right in the heart of the most affected areas.

Sixteen of Harris's Carpetright shops were damaged in the 2011 riots, and the burnt-out shell of the Tottenham store in North London became one of the defining images of the worst riots in living memory. More than 30 families lived above the classical, 1930s art-deco store, and on the Wednesday after the riots, Harris got them all together and gave each £2,500 and a promise to fit out their homes with new carpets. 'They were left with nothing,' he said.

His roots are in Peckham (hence his choice of Lord Harris of Peckham when he was awarded his peerage in 1996) in South London where his father Charles ran his market stall in Rye Lane. He knew his father had been a soldier in the war, but it was only years afterwards that he discovered he was actually something of a hero: Charles Harris enlisted in the ranks at the outbreak of War in 1939, and was commissioned in 1945 after he led a charge on a German pill-box, for which he won the Military Cross. He later serviced in Palestine as an acting captain. Phil commissioned a sculpture of him which is now in Harris Manchester College.

Besides business and his family, his two consuming interests are politics and horses. He was deputy chairman of the Conservative Party Treasurers, and became close to Baroness Thatcher, who he still sees, and to John Major, one of his closest friends, who he reckons is the most under-rated prime minister since the War. 'He left behind the healthiest economy in Britain's history, won the 1992 election against all the odds, but never gets enough credit for it'. Phil was one of the first supporters of David Cameron and backed his campaign for leadership of the party.

Lord Harris celebrates with one of his Academies

Tottenham store after the August 2011 riots

His successes in the equestrian world have been equally spectacular. He and his wife Pauline owned Philco, Sportsman and Midnight Madness, all ridden by David Broome, and generally thought to be among the greatest show-jumpers of all time. Broome, a professional rider was banned from the Olympics in his best years, and when the rules changed he finished fourth in Seoul in 1988 and only ninth in Barcelona. After a gap of 12 years, Harris is now back with three horses in the current British Olympic squad, two of which, ridden by Tina Fletcher and Scott Brash, have a good chance of a medal.

A gold would be a fitting contribution to Her Majesty's Jubilee year, from a man who has already given a great deal during her reign.

Photograph by Rex Features

www.carpetright.co.uk

PORT OF SPAIN

Many of us have grown up recognising Her Majesty Queen Elizabeth II as the symbol of the United Kingdom and of the quintessential monarch. Her reign has spanned my entire lifetime, and yet Her Majesty continues to embrace her roles as the Head of the British monarchy, Head of State of the United Kingdom and Head of the Commonwealth with the same enthusiasm as she did when she took to the throne.

Queen Elizabeth II has, with grace and aplomb, managed to successfully carry the British monarchy forward into the 21st century. The monarchy today is relevant, respected and greatly loved, not only by the people of Great Britain and Northern Ireland, but around the world. This is in large part due to Her Majesty's unflagging efforts to keep the monarchy modern, open and fully engaged.

From 2010 to 2011 I held the position of chairperson-in-office of the Commonwealth, and it was during this time that I was able to truly appreciate the part played by Queen Elizabeth II as the Head of the Commonwealth. She stands as a powerful symbol of unity and longevity at the head of this organisation which she herself has described as "the original worldwide web"'. It brings together a cross-section of 54 countries from around the world, seeking to unify the plethora of religions, ethnicities and cultures encompassed therein. It is her presence at the helm of the modern Commonwealth which lends such a strong sense of familial linkage and heritage to the Commonwealth. Her dedication and deep-rooted sense of duty to the Commonwealth is invaluable to all members and to the organisation itself.

During my office in 2011, the Commonwealth theme was Women Leaders as Agents of Change. The theme motivated me to pursue a number of initiatives to promote the importance of women in leadership roles. As such, Queen Elizabeth II is indeed one of the most inspirational and significant woman leaders in history. She has remained an unshakeable source of continuity, strength, dignity and compassion for the British people and has weathered both good times and bad with pride, diligence, and above all, a profound love of her subjects.

As the first female prime minister of my country, I respect Her Majesty not only for her longevity but, more importantly, for her extraordinary ability as an intrepid and committed woman leader. I therefore wish Her Majesty my deepest and most heartfelt congratulations on the occasion of her Diamond Jubilee.

Hon. Kamla Persad-Bissessar

Prime Minister

THAILAND

On this historic and auspicious occasion of the Diamond Jubilee of Her Majesty Queen Elizabeth II's accession to the throne, their Majesties King Bhumibol Adulyadej and Queen Sirikit of Thailand have sent their heartfelt congratulations and best wishes for the happiness and well-being of Her Majesty, His Royal Highness the Duke of Edinburgh and all the members of the Royal Family, as well as for the continued progress and prosperity of the United Kingdom and her people.

Throughout a remarkable 60-year reign, Her Majesty Queen Elizabeth II's steadfast dedication to many deserving and charitable causes and her unwavering commitment to the well-being of her subjects has earned her enormous respect and admiration in the United Kingdom, the Commonwealth and beyond. During Her Majesty's reign, the cordial relations between our two Royal families have also been cherished.

On this milestone occasion may I, on behalf of the Royal Thai Embassy and the Thai Community in the United Kingdom, humbly extend my sincerest best wishes to Her Majesty Queen Elizabeth II and all the members of the Royal Family, as well as for the continued close and cordial relations between the United Kingdom and Thailand and their peoples.

Long may she reign.

Kitti Wasinondh

Ambassador of Thailand to the United Kingdom

POLAND

Your Majesty,

It is my great privilege and honour to present my sincere congratulations marking Your Majesty's Diamond Jubilee.

The past 60 years of Her Majesty's reign have witnessed unique developments and events across the globe, and the 2012 celebrations are a wonderful culmination of this remarkable time.

Throughout your reign an ever-strengthening relationship between Poland and the United Kingdom has been endorsed, a testimony for what we hope will continue into the future.

On this occasion, I wish to convey my heartfelt congratulations and best wishes for the years to come.

With assurances of my highest consideration,

Barbara Tuge-Erecińska

Ambassador of the Republic of Poland to the Court of St James's

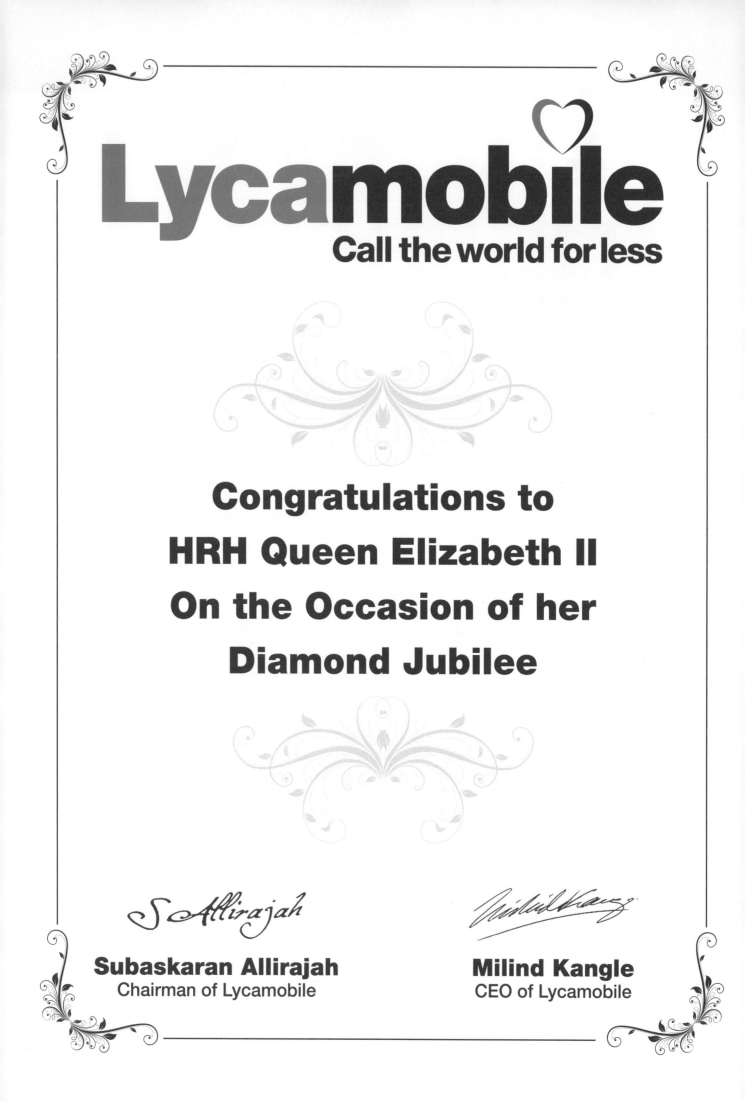

Lycamobile
Call the world for less

Congratulations to HRH Queen Elizabeth II On the Occasion of her Diamond Jubilee

Subaskaran Allirajah
Chairman of Lycamobile

Milind Kangle
CEO of Lycamobile

David Faul

The National Memorial Arboretum

Barely a decade after it first opened, this key memorial for Britain's soldiers has become an important part of national life

Since it was officially opened in May 2001, the National Memorial Arboretum in Lichfield, Staffordshire has become one of the most important sites in the United Kingdom for remembering and recognising the sacrifices of those who gave their lives serving in the Armed Forces. It is now visited by thousands each year in Remembrance.

The 150-acre site, managed and maintained by The Royal British Legion, contains over 50,000 trees and 200 memorials dedicated to those who lost their lives serving their country. More than 300,000 people visit the site annually, with many coming to visit for the daily service of Remembrance held in the Millennium Chapel of Peace. There is no charge to patrons entering the Arboretum and it is open every   >>

The Royal National Lifeboat Institution memorial, with poppies in the foreground, at the National Memorial Arboretum

"Two hundred events are held annually at the Arboretum, with Her Majesty among those who pay their respects"

Her Majesty the Queen at the opening of the Armed Forces Memorial, 2011

day of the year with the exception of Christmas Day. Two hundred special events are held annually at the Arboretum, with Her Majesty the Queen and other royal guests among those who regularly pay their respects.

A focal point

The idea for the Arboretum was conceived by Commander David Childs CBE in 1988. Following an Appeal launched by then-Prime Minister John Major in 1994, a generous donation of land was made by Redland Aggregates materials company (now Lafarge) and construction was

given the go-ahead. The Arboretum and its purpose has received high praise from visitors, notably from the Duke of Cambridge, Prince William. On Armistice Day last year, the future king remarked that "In just a few years, the National Memorial Arboretum has become the focal point for the Remembrance of our nation's heroes".

Her Majesty the Queen is also a frequent visitor to the Arboretum. Recently, on 21 July 2011, she attended a service dedicated to the 112 members of the Armed Forces who lost their lives in combat during 2010. As the names of the personnel were being read aloud, the Queen and the

Fotocapricorn; MoD; National Memorial Arboretum

A place to reflect

Perhaps the most meaningful praise for the work of the National Memorial Arboretum came last year from Kate Darbyshire, who lost husband Steven after he was fatally wounded in Afghanistan. "The Armed Forces Memorial provides a permanent record of the brave men and women who have given their lives to protect the safety of others. The memorial is a place of quiet reflection away from the hustle and bustle of urban life – the beauty of the structure and the simplicity of the carved names on the Portland stone depicts the loss of so many young lives," she remarked.

synonymous with year-round Remembrance," he says. In the three months before he spoke, Kennedy saw 10 new memorials enter the Arboretum; among those dedicated in that time were to the Women's Auxiliary Air Force and the Royal Navy Lifeboat Institution.

Fundraising

Realising that the Arboretum was catering for more and more visitors every year, an Appeal was launched by Prince William in April 2009 to raise £8 million, later £12 million, in funding to expand and develop the Arboretum. Most recently, in aid of the Appeal, the Duke and Duchess of Cambridge hosted a black-tie reception and dinner as part of their itinerary for marking last year's Armistice Day. The funds generated from the Appeal will go towards constructing a Veterans' Pavilion, which will accommodate functions and events, as well as a new entrance and a Remembrance and Learning Centre.

Among the key memorials already in place at the Arboretum is the Armed Forces Memorial, which is dedicated to those who have been killed on duty as a result of terrorist action since the end of the Second World War. Opened by the Queen in a special service in 2007 that was led by the then-Archbishop of Canterbury Dr Rowan Williams, more than 16,000 names are inscribed on the memorial, with more added each year in June. In a specially-designed feature of the memorial, the sun shines on the wreath at the centre of the well at 11am during every Armistice Day mass. The sculptor, Ian Rank-Broadley, had earlier in his career created the effigy of the Queen that has been used on sterling coins since 2008.

The Basra memorial, dedicated to the 178 UK servicemen, one Minister of Defence official, and foreign soldiers >>

families of fallen soldiers placed wreaths at the bottom of the Armed Forces memorial, which had been engraved with the names of the dead.

The Basra Wall: A tribute to those lost in conflict, built by their comrades and relocated to the Aboretum for loved ones to remember (top). Prince William pays his respects at the Armed Forces Memorial site (above)

Room for Remembrance

Accommodating memorials is a key aspect of the National Memorial Arboretum's work today. With 165 in place at the beginning of 2011, the Arboretum experienced a record year for the opening for new memorials – more than 40 were unveiled throughout the year. The Arboretum's curator, Paul Kennedy, said at the start of the year that new applications are received warmly. "The increase in memorial applications is warmly welcomed. It's just 10 years since the Arboretum first opened its gates and, in this short time, we have become a nationally important site and a place

Pertemps Network, the award

be supporting HM The

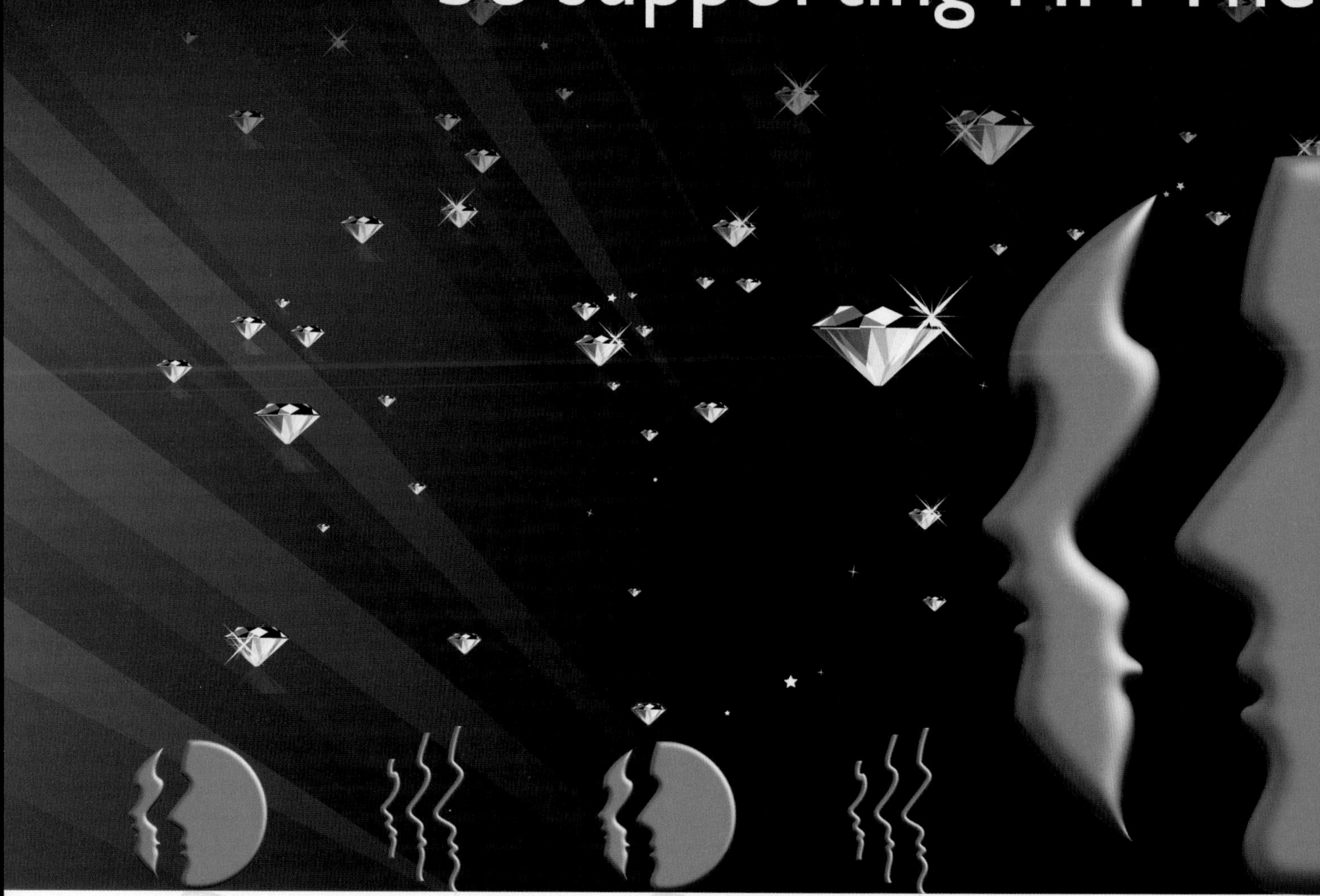

GO AWARD
SCOTLAND

THE SUNDAY TIMES
TOP 100 COMPANIES

BEST COMPANIES
STATUS

DIVERSITY PLUS
AWARD

Pertemps came into existence when Her Majesty had been in power for just nine years. In that time we, like Her Majesty, have seen transformations take place.

Her reign has seen many changes in all areas. From technology and medicine through to world politics and the economy, Her Majesty has seen:

- Britain under 12 Prime Ministers
- The discovery of oil in the North Sea
- The western world's first female Prime Minister
- The introduction of the decimal currency
- Britain joining the European Community

- Concorde making trans-Atlantic flights
- The world's first test tube baby
- Numerous worldwide conflicts
- The opening of the Channel Tunnel
- The marriages of members of the Royal Family

In the time since Pertemps began we too have seen many changes in our business:

- Growing from a single branch to over 200 branches across 90 towns and cities in the UK
- Becoming one of the largest independent recruitment consultancies in Britain
- Having over 20,000 workers out on placement each week
- 2010 saw the most successful year in our company history with turnover increasing by 24% on the previous year
- Working with many blue chip clients across both the public and private sector
- Winning numerous awards and accolades as an employer including the Coutts Family Business award, and being named one of The Sunday Times 100 Best Companies to work for, for five consecutive years

winning recruiters are proud to
Queen's Diamond Jubilee

| BEST RECRUITMENT COMPANY TO WORK FOR | "LEADING THE WAY" REMPLOY AWARD | THE SUNDAY TIMES TOP TRACK 250 | REC "ONE IN A MILLION" |

What the Monarch and successful businesses have in common, is that to continue and grow both recognise the importance of embracing and accepting change.

Throughout good times and hard times The Queen has always shown a remarkable level of strength and compassion, inspiring not just her country and people but the world to have confidence in her.

As Her Majesty celebrates 60 years on the throne, Pertemps Network would like to extend our congratulations to her on her lengthy and successful reign, keeping Britain strong and proud through both times of conflict and times of success. Long may she continue to reign over us and we hope the Diamond Jubilee is an 'annus mirabilis'.

Tim Watts, Pertemps Lifetime President

www.pertemps.co.uk

Meriden Hall, Main Road, Meriden,
Warwickshire CV7 7PT. Tel: 01676 525000

Celebrating 50 YEARS IN RECRUITMENT

who died under British command, was originally erected in the Iraqi city by the soldiers from the 37 Armoured Engineer Squadron in 2006, and stood outside the headquarters of the Multi-National Division. However, it was later dismantled and the brass plaques from the monument were brought to Britain to be displayed in the Arboretum. The dedication ceremony was attended by the Duke of Gloucester and then-Prime Minister Gordon Brown.

The Far East Prisoners of War Building is another prominent memorial at the venue. The monument commemorates the 55,000 Service personnel who were

The Shot at Dawn Memorial remembers the 306 British and Commonwealth soldiers executed for desertion and cowardice in WWI (top). Among the most visited monuments is the Millennium Chapel of Peace and Forgiveness (above)

captured and killed by the Japanese during the Second World War. Opened on 15 August 2005 (the 60th anniversary of VJ Day), the building contains archived footage and news reels depicting the lives of these prisoners during the war; next to it is the original memorial built by some of the prisoners themselves at Changi Jail in Singapore to commemorate their fallen comrades.

Soldiers shot for cowardice or desertion during the First World War – typically underage, suffering post-traumatic stress or shell shock and executed without a fair trial – are also remembered at the 'Shot at Dawn' memorial. In 2006, British and Irish soldiers who were executed in this way during the war were given a mass pardon. As a symbol of the executions, the names are listed on stakes arranged on in the shape of a Greek theatre, to signify the tragedy they represent. Among those shot was Private Herbert Burden, aged 17, who was executed in Ypres in 1915. A statue of the private now accompanies the stakes.

Among the most visited monuments is the Millennium Chapel of Peace and Forgiveness, at which a moment of silence for those who have lost their lives in Service is >>

National Memorial Arboretum

Congratulations on your Diamond Jubilee, Your Majesty

At MetLife, we pride ourselves on offering innovative insurance, retirement and savings products for millions of people around the world.

As the leading life insurer in the United States we've been providing for life's uncertainties for 145 years. And that's exactly what we've been doing in the UK for the last five years.

We take great pleasure in expressing our congratulations to her Majesty the Queen on this, her Diamond Jubilee.

To find out more about MetLife speak to your financial adviser or visit **www.metlife.co.uk**

"*The Polish Armed Forces Memorial is an educational aid for those not familiar with the contribution of the allied forces*"

National Memorial Arboretum

The Polish Armed Forces Memorial (pictured) was introduced to the Arboretum in 2009 to recognise the lives given by the Polish fighters in the Second World War

held daily. Built in November 2000, the chapel signifies the desire for peace and celebration as the world enters the new millennium. The features of the chapel's exterior are meant to represent the design used by early Christians in Britain 1700 years ago. Inside the building itself and behind the alter hang three crosses. One is the Sword of Sacrifice – seen at every Commonwealth War Graves cemetery; the other two are made of elm that was destroyed by Dutch Elm Disease. These represent the thieves' crosses.

Some memorials in the Arboretum were erected to remember the contribution of foreign service personnel. One is the Polish Armed Forces Memorial, which was introduced to the National Memorial Arboretum in September 2009 to recognise the lives given by Polish fighters during the Second World War. The dedication of the memorial was met with praise from the Polish Defence Minister, Boguslaw Klitch, who in 2010 awarded the Wojska Polskiegomedal to the Arboretum's curator Paul Kennedy, chief executive Charlie Baggot Jewitt and volunteer John Bryan for "popularising the Polish Armed Forces Abroad". On receiving

his medal, Kennedy took the opportunity to reiterate the contribution made by soldiers from that country. "The Polish Armed Forces Memorial is both a focus for Remembrance and an important educational aid for those who are not >>

Recognising the effort

As a reward for their hard work in making a success of the Arboretum, in 2010, volunteers at the Arboretum received The Queen's Award for

Voluntary Service – the equivalent of an MBE. The near 140 volunteers were granted the honour in a special ceremony and received a piece of commemorative crystal and a certificate personally signed by the Queen as recognition of their hard work. The award was presented to the volunteers by James Hawley, Her Majesty's representative in Staffordshire. The award was created in 2002 to mark the Queen's Golden Jubilee.

AT HER MAJESTY'S SERVICE

FOR 60 YEARS

RSA send our warmest congratulations to Her Majesty The Queen on her Diamond Jubilee.

We share a long and proud history with the British Monarchy. From the two Royal Charters granted to us by King George I, to our donations to St Catherine's College Oxford, where The Queen laid the first stone, our affiliation with the Monarchy is based on strong foundations, built over centuries.

We are proud to celebrate this momentous anniversary, which marks the extraordinary commitment and dedication The Queen has shown to the United Kingdom and the Commonwealth.

RSA employees from across the globe wish The Queen a happy and successful Jubilee year.

"The Arboretum has become one of the most well-known sites not only in the UK but throughout the world, too"

The entire National Memorial Arboretum site (pictured) is surrounded by woodland, wildlife and lakes in Staffordshire

familiar with the significant contribution of the allied Polish forces," he remarked.

The Arboretum also contains memorials to those who died on duty as police officers and as fire service and ambulance personnel, and COPS (Care of Police Survivors) holds an annual service dedicated to those who died on duty. The charity says that although the service itself can be a trying experience, a weekend of family activities takes place around the Arboretum, and it is also meant to be a fun occasion where families can interact and enjoy themselves. The charity, Police Roll of Honour Trust, which remembers those who have died serving on duty, has said that it is deeply committed to its goal of establishing a memorial at the Arboretum and registered its intent with the Charity Commission.

Upcoming memorials

Construction of the Falklands Memorial is almost complete and will be dedicated in May 2012, and members of the Nottingham branch of the Parachute Regiment Association are currently fundraising for a commemorative bronze statue. The Arboretum has recently taken the

step of bringing Mike Marylon, a cabinet member on Staffordshire County Council, on board to help shape future plans for the memorial's development and raise its international profile. Aside from the memorials, the Arboretum is home to a wide abundance of wildlife, including woodpeckers, owls, buntings, skylarks and otters, all of which enjoy the site's woodland, grassland and wetland environments.

The Arboretum has become an all-inclusive focal point for Remembrance, and the Appeal for more funding is evidence of that. Attracting visitors that range from families and veterans to historians and tourists, the Arboretum is now at the centre of much of the country's Remembrance activity, and plays a vital role in keeping the memories alive of those who made the ultimate sacrifice for their country. Thanks to the constant care and maintenance provided by its staff and volunteers, and the publicity generated by Prince William and other members of the Royal Family and public officials, the Arboretum has become one of the most well-known sites not only in the UK but throughout the world, too. ■

National Memorial Arboretum

On behalf of the Mayor and the people of Sunderland, I would like to congratulate Your Majesty on the occasion of your Diamond Jubilee.

As a city with a proud history and heritage we have been honoured to welcome Your Majesty to Sunderland on a number of occasions during your long and illustrious reign.

We were overjoyed when in 1992 you chose to honour Sunderland with city status as part of celebrations to mark the 40th year of your reign.

In 2002 we were delighted to welcome Your Majesty and His Royal Highness the Duke of Edinburgh back to our city, to open Sunderland Museum & Winter Gardens and newly restored Mowbray Park.

We were equally thrilled when you and His Royal Highness agreed to open our brand new eco-friendly Washington School in November 2009.

These visits certainly meant a great deal to the people of Sunderland, who turned out in their thousands to cheer your Majesty. We hope they hold fond memories for you and His Royal Highness too.

We were delighted to be invited to be part of this publication as the people of this city have a long and proud history of supporting the Royal British Legion.

More than 40,000 Sunderland men and women served in World War II and the city still has higher than average numbers of servicemen and women.

Sadly, this has also meant suffering higher losses in recent conflicts. But the determination of the people of this city to honour those who have made the ultimate sacrifice has never been stronger.

The city's Remembrance Parade is the largest outside of London. Just last year a remarkable group of Sunderland people who lost loved ones in recent years, raised funds to build a memorial wall as a permanent tribute to Sunderland men and women who have lost their lives since World War II. This lasting legacy to those who gave their lives for their country was dedicated in a moving service on Armistice Day 2011.

We have also been proud to welcome other members of The Royal Family to the city in recent years, including Her Royal Highness The Princess Royal, who opened our fantastic Sunderland Aquatic Centre, and HRH The Earl of Wessex who laid a wreath at our Remembrance Service in 2007.

This year we have been delighted to host events to celebrate Your Majesty's Diamond Jubilee, including taking part in the lighting of beacons across the country.

Your Majesty, we in Sunderland want to wish you well as you celebrate 60 glorious years on the throne. We wish you many more happy years to come.

Paul Watson

Councillor Paul Watson
Leader of Sunderland City Council

AMBALA®

Since it was established in London in 1965, Ambala has become one of the most prestigious Asian confectionery and savoury brands. It is undoubtedly the driving energy and unique recipes of the founder, Mohammad Ali Khan and his uncompromising insistence on only using premium quality ingredients that has ensured Ambala's unrivalled quality, taste and continued success.

It was a passionate entrepreneurial spirit that inspired Mohammad Ali Khan to begin creating his *"works of art"* from a flat opposite the Shaftesbury Theatre in High Holborn, London in 1964, and supply local Indian restaurants, including the famous *Veeraswamy's* of Regent Street with exquisite and delicious after dinner desserts. By 1965, he had opened his first store in Euston, London, naming it after the town in India where he was born and the rest, as they say, is history.

Ambala's reputation grew rapidly especially amongst the burgeoning Asian community and before long, scenes of queuing customers stretching from the store, halfway to Euston station was not an uncommon site. Within a short time, Ambala's position as the nation's premier Asian confectioner was established and remains so to this day, with ever-increasing customers among the British, European and American public. Asked about his motivations, Mohammed Ali Khan replies simply: *"I have a God-given gift which I wish to share with others and see it as my duty to serve humanity."*

A steady period of growth saw the opening of Ambala outlets throughout the country and abroad. As Ambala's cosmopolitan customer base grew ever larger within the UK and its reputation spread internationally, Mohammed Ali Khan identified the need for an alternative supply stream, and in 2004, Ambala went online with the launch of its website. *"I wanted to reach those loyal customers who were unable to visit our stores easily"*, says Mohammad Ali Khan.

Another milestone worthy of mention is Ambala's accreditation of the BRC Global standard in Food Safety which was awarded in 2011 at the Company's new facility in Welwyn Garden City, Hertfordshire.

As we begin 2012 and an exciting Summer in the Capital beckons, Mohammad Ali Khan's spirit and driving energy remains undiminished: *"Ambala has some very interesting new inventions that will be launched this year in time to commemorate the Queen's Diamond Jubilee, including a very special free gift for every online order placed from the 7th May - 15th July 2012. On behalf of Ambala, we would like to congratulate Her Majesty on her Diamond Jubilee. Long live our gracious Queen."*

Please visit us at _www.ambala.co.uk._

Against All Odds

At 28 years old, Mark Ormrod's story is an inspiration. Now he is playing his part to raise awareness about the work of The Royal British Legion

Former Royal Marine, Mark Ormrod, is gearing up to give two uplifting talks soon. Both speeches will be delivered to clients he has attracted to his newly formed motivational speaking company.

It's easy to see why the former marine who served in Iraq in 2003 and Afghanistan in 2007 as well as on tours of the Mediterranean and Norway, is attracting new customers – his story, after all, is an inspirational one.

Finding an open door

While on foot patrol in Afghanistan on Christmas Eve 2007, Mark stepped on a buried landmine. The blast resulted in him having both of his legs amputated above the knee and his right arm amputated above the elbow.

Rather than allow his injuries to determine the outcome of the rest of his life, Mark made the decision to seek as much help as he could and he found an open door at The Royal British Legion. Since then, he has gone on to become an operations and welfare assistant with The Royal Marines Association and helps others try to come to terms with life changing injuries, similar to those he suffered himself. "In my role as a charity worker with the Royal Marines, I come across people who could be helped by The Royal British Legion. I'm a qualified volunteer case worker for the Legion and whenever I am asked to contribute, I do it because they have helped me out so much in the past."

Mark helped launch the Poppy Appeal in 2009 alongside then-eight-year-old Lydia Cross who lost her legs to meningitis in 2003. A year later, he embarked on a gruelling 3600 mile run across the United States with fellow former Service men from the British and American forces to raise awareness and money for injured troops.

Getting the message across

In 2009, Mark also published his book, *Man Down* – a brutally honest memoir of his own experience and how he faced up to the greatest battle of his life following his injuries. His rousing story and the profile he has generated has helped The Royal British Legion to heighten awareness in the public domain of its work. "I think there was a

"There is no discriminaton – as long as you served seven days or more, you get the help that you need"

Mark provides inspiration for others learning to adapt to life-changing injuries (above): The former marine on duty in Afghanistan (right)

misconception about The Royal British Legion for a long time," Mark admits. "The first thing that popped into many people's mind was old clubs with retired veterans – I wasn't aware of the support they give to people and the welfare they provide. Today, the fact that a large amount of injured, younger guys support the Legion is making a real impact when it comes to raising awareness of what the Legion is all about and the effect it can have on people's lives. I believe the message is starting to get across now."

"There is a lot of support out there for the Legion because guys like myself who served and are serving in Afghanistan are at the forefront of everyone's minds, but those who served during other conflicts, such as The Falklands, Bosnia or Kosovo, need just as much help as we do. I think one of the best things about The Royal British Legion is that there is no discrimination about where and when someone served to determine the help they receive – as long as you served for seven days or more, you get the help that you need." ■

ARMENIA

On the occasion of the 60th anniversary of Her Majesty's accession to the throne, the Armenian people and I would like to extend our warmest congratulations and best wishes to Her Majesty Queen Elizabeth II, the Royal Family and the people of the United Kingdom of Great Britain and Northern Ireland.

Through her activities Her Majesty has contributed to the prosperity of the British society over six decades, consolidating the highest universal values and preserving the best traditions of the Royal Crown. During her reign and her active involvement in state and public spheres, Her Majesty Queen Elizabeth II has manifested characteristic features of a compassionate individual with strong willpower.

In a constantly changing and unstable world Queen Elizabeth II, as a virtuous and noble state figure, has gained deep respect due to her devotion to spiritual values and national traditions not only from the subjects of the United Kingdom and the Commonwealth, but also the international community, becoming the embodiment of faith and dignity. She harmoniously combines the image of not only an exemplary monarch, but also of a graceful woman, caring mother, gentle and loving grandmother, yielding admiration in people's hearts.

I am glad to have had the opportunity to meet and have an interesting conversation with Her Majesty, in particular about British Armenian friendship – friendship that is based on the common values of our peoples and their unwavering faith in a peaceful and bright future.

We wish Her Majesty strong health, vigour and vitality in her future undertakings, as well as happy and peaceful days surrounded by the love and respect of the Royal Family and her subjects.

God Save the Queen!

Serzh Sargsyan

President of Armenia

SLOVAK REPUBLIC

On behalf of the people of the Slovak Republic, as well as in my own name, please allow me to express my sincere congratulations to Her Majesty the Queen on celebrating her Diamond Jubilee this year. With the highest respect for her 60 years on the throne, I would like to wish Her Majesty the Queen many more productive years, sound health and happiness. Allow me to take this opportunity to emphasise the high standards of amicable and allied relation between our two countries, which have been acknowledged by the state visit of Her Majesty to Slovakia.

Congratulations once again and Happy Anniversary.

Ivan Gašparovič

President of the Slovak Republic

CYPRUS

I wish to extend my warmest congratulations to Her Majesty Queen Elizabeth II on the 60th anniversary of her reign.

As part of the Commonwealth family of nations and as an EU partner, the Republic of Cyprus shares with the United Kingdom of Great Britain and Northern Ireland common goals for peace, security, stability and prosperity for our nations. In pursuing these noble objectives, we will continue to rely on Her Majesty's valuable support and moral example. Her dedication and commitment over the years to our shared goals has been highly appreciated and valued. On behalf of the people and the Government of the Republic of Cyprus, I wish Her Majesty happiness, good health and a long reign.

Demetris Christofias

President of the Republic of Cyprus

Taking a good look at Specsavers

The optical company known for its sense of humour and 'Should've gone to Specsavers' tv commercials is a great British retail success story that the nation should be proud of.

Although now the largest privately owned optical company in the world, Specsavers' beginnings were humble indeed.

Founded in 1984 by optometrists Doug and Dame Mary Perkins, who met at university in Cardiff, the business began with two part-time staff – both of whom are still with the company – in the couple's spare bedroom using a table-tennis table as a desk. Glasses were posted to their first few stores from a letterbox along the road.

Little did they think then that their small optical business would, in less than three decades, expand to 1,650 stores, spanning 10 countries across two continents and employing more than 30,000 staff.

With stores in the Netherlands, Sweden, Norway, Denmark, Finland, Spain, Australia and New Zealand, as well as 700 in the UK and Ireland, Specsavers has become a great British retail success story.

Doug was born in Llanelli, Wales, the son of a policeman, while Dame Mary hails from Bristol. Her father was an optician and it is from him that she developed her passion for eyecare. Dame Mary made it her mission to revolutionise the optical industry and make fashionable eyewear affordable for everyone.

The early years

In the early 1980s the UK government deregulated some professions, including opticians, allowing them to advertise their products and services for the first time. Doug and Dame Mary seized this opportunity and opened their first Specsavers Opticians – offering value-for-money, quality eyecare – in Guernsey and Bristol. These were soon followed by stores in Plymouth, Swansea and Bath. The Perkinses wanted the company to be seen as being as trustworthy as a local independent optician but benefiting from the huge buying power of a national company, meaning savings could be passed on to the customer.

As opticians themselves, the Perkinses realised that for opticians to really feel a part of their business, they had to have a stake in its ownership and profits. Much research led them to develop the groundbreaking 'joint-venture partnership' model which is the basis of the company's success and continues to thrive today.

'We were certain right from the beginning that the best and only business model for retail optics was based on partnership; a partnership which brings together local opticians owning their own stores, committed to delivering best value to their customers; a partnership providing the highest standards of professional care supported by world-class business support services,' says Dame Mary.

Fashionable and affordable

Specsavers signalled the dawn of a new age in optics, based on high volume and low and clear pricing – the price displayed on the frames was inclusive of lenses in what Specsavers called Complete Price. This value-for-money approach meant that for the first time, people were able to view

Bringing sight to Africa

Specsavers dispensing assistant Chanel McGarry meets Her Majesty the Queen in Epsom

SHOULD'VE GONE TO SPECSAVERS

Specsavers is renowned for its humorous award-winning TV ads

Specsavers' flagship store in Tottenham Court Road, London

glasses not just as a necessity but also as a fashion accessory. This was helped in no small part by Specsavers pioneering the introduction of two for one – buy one pair of glasses and the second pair is free. Accepted very much as the norm in optical retailing today, Specsavers' two for one was seen as revolutionary when it was introduced in 1990 and has been much imitated by its competitors over the years.

Family values

Standing still is not an option for this dynamic British company, as it continues to lead by innovation and to put its customers first. As well as being the leading provider of glasses and contact lenses, it also offers a hearing service from more than 400 locations.

Specsavers is still family-owned, led by Doug and Dame Mary Perkins, honoured in 2007 for services to buisness and charity. Son John is

joint managing director and both daughters, Julie and Cathy, work in senior roles in the business.

Voted Britain's Most Trusted Optician* for 10 years running, Specsavers' vision and values are not just a corporate statement on a wall. They firmly believe that they are there to provide a service to the community. Dame Mary's passion for 'giving something back' extends to numerous charities and good causes with which the company works, including Guide Dogs, Hearing Dogs for Deaf people, Vision Aid Overseas, Sound Seekers, the anti-bullying charity Kidscape and the road safety charity Brake. Stores support hundreds of local causes, ranging from fundraising for hospices and community groups to providing free sight tests for taxi drivers in London and high-visibility vests for schoolchildren in Scotland and Wales.

Says Dame Mary: 'Our belief in partnership extends beyond the boundaries of the Specsavers family and applies to everyone we come into contact with. As members of what has become known as 'the green blood club' we believe in treating others as we would like to be treated ourselves and in developing meaningful and respectful relationships with our customers, our people, our store director partners and our communities. At Specsavers, we want our customers to be customers for life.'

Reader's Digest Trusted Brands survey 2002-2011

Crowning Glory

– Memories of the Coronation

Sixty years ago the nation's hearts and minds were captured by the Queen's Coronation. We look at what happened on that unforgettable day

The Duke of Edinburgh pays homage to his wife, the newly crowned Queen Elizabeth II, during her Coronation ceremony held at Westminster Abbey

The Diamond Jubilee is not only an opportunity to celebrate the 60th anniversary of the Queen's reign, but also to fondly remember the collective celebrations that took place throughout Britain and the Commonwealth during the Coronation of the Queen in 1953. This historical and monumental occasion captivated the nation at a time of renewed optimism and a sense of possibility.

The Coronation

The Coronation of Queen Elizabeth II took place in Westminster Abbey in London on 2 June 1953, more than a year after the accession, which gave an appropriate period of mourning following the death of her father, George VI.

The crowning of the Sovereign is an ancient ceremony that has taken place at Westminster Abbey for over 900 years. Dr Geoffrey Fisher, the then-Archbishop of Canterbury, conducted the ceremony; and representatives from the Commons, past prime ministers, leading citizens of other Commonwealth countries and foreign heads of state, were all present.

During the Coronation ceremony, which was attended by some 8000 guests, Elizabeth II swore an oath to uphold the laws of her nations and, specifically to govern the Church of England.

She was given the orb, representing the Sovereign's role as defender of the faith; the sceptre, representing >>

Getty Images

Christianity; the rod of mercy, symbolising the Holy Ghost; and the Coronation ring, which is often referred to as the "wedding ring of England". Attached to the shoulders of her dress, Elizabeth II wore the Robe of State, an ornate, hand-woven silk, velvet cloak, lined with Canadian ermine.

The Archbishop placed St Edward's Crown, which was made in 1661, on Queen Elizabeth's head to complete the ceremony. A roar of "God save the Queen!" rang out and gun salutes were fired as crowds cheered. The Archbishop and fellow bishops then paid homage to the Queen, who went on to declare: "Throughout all my life, and with all my heart, I shall strive to be worthy of your trust."

TV moment

Although the Coronation ceremony of Elizabeth II followed tradition and was similar to the Coronations of other kings and queens, the new Queen requested that the ceremony be televised. At the time, there was much debate within the British Cabinet, with Prime Minister Winston Churchill opposed to the idea of televising the event.

Despite these reservations, it was the first Coronation ceremony to be televised. It was also broadcast on radio in 39 languages by 750 commentators stationed in Westminster Abbey. As the world's first major international event to be broadcast on television, for the first time in history, British citizens around the globe witnessed first-hand this auspicious occasion.

It is estimated that more than 20 million people watched the BBC coverage of the Coronation. Many people crowded around neighbours' TV sets as for some it was their first time to watch television. In order to make sure that Canadians could see it on the same day, English Electric Canberra planes flew film of the ceremony across the Atlantic to the Canadian Broadcasting Corporation.

Crowd pleaser

Villages, towns and cities across the UK were decorated in red, white and blue bunting in celebration, and in London, the roads were packed with people waiting to see the Royal procession.

Despite heavy rain on the day, some three million spectators gathered to view the procession; some having camped out overnight in order to secure a prime view of the Queen and the rest of the monarchy. >>

Getty Images

"Despite heavy rain on the day, some three million spectators gathered to view the procession, some having camped overnight"

From left: The Queen and her retinue at Westminster Abbey after the Coronation ceremony. Gladstone Terrace, Northampton, which won the prize of Best Decorated Street in the town

From left: The Queen in her carriage passing through Trafalgar Square on her way to the Abbey. Queen Elizabeth II and the Duke of Edinburgh wave at the crowds from the balcony at Buckingham Palace on the momentous day

So large was the procession to Westminster Abbey that businessmen and country squires offered their services to assist the coachmen in transporting dignitaries to the Abbey.

The first Royal coach left Buckingham Palace and moved down the Mall, which was lined with flag-waving, cheering crowds. It was followed by the Irish State Coach carrying Elizabeth II and the Queen Mother, which proceeded from Buckingham Palace, through Trafalgar Square towards the Abbey.

Keepsakes

Many commemorative souvenirs were produced to mark the occasion, including a special set of four postage stamps. As with the Coronation of George VI, acorns shed from oaks in Windsor Castle were shipped around the Commonwealth and planted in parks to grow into what are known as Royal Oaks or Coronation Oaks.

News that Edmund Hillary and Tenzing Norgay had reached the summit of Mount Everest arrived in Britain on the day of the Queen's Coronation and the media were quick to dub it: "a Coronation gift for the new Queen".

When the Coronation ceremony was over, Queen Elizabeth returned to Buckingham Palace, acknowledging and waving to the thousands of people that lined the streets. Crowds gathered to catch a glimpse of the Queen and other members of the Royal Family as they waved from the balcony of the Palace.

Despite the overcast weather conditions, the Royal Air Force marked the occasion by flying past the Mall, and a fireworks display lit up the skies above Victoria Embankment.

Global celebrations

After the official Coronation, the Queen visited Scotland, Northern Ireland and Wales. Across the Queen's realms and the rest of the Commonwealth, Coronation celebrations were held with great fanfare and pageantry.

In London, the Queen hosted a Coronation luncheon, for which the recipe, Coronation chicken, was devised. Street parties were organised all over the United Kingdom and the Coronation Cup Football Tournament was held at Hampden Park, Glasgow in May to mark the occasion.

In the United States, Coronation parties were mounted; one in New York City attended by the Queen's uncle and

"Crowds gathered to catch a glimpse of the Queen and the Royal Family as they waved from the balcony of the Palace"

aunt, the Duke and Duchess of Windsor. In Canada, military tattoos, horse races, parades, and fireworks displays were staged. On Parliament Hill in Ottawa, the Queen's Coronation speech was broadcast. In Newfoundland, sweets were dropped to children by the Royal Canadian Air Force, and in Quebec, 400,000 people turned out in Montreal to watch the Coronation ceremony.

The Queen Elizabeth II Coronation Medal was presented to thousands of recipients throughout the Queen's countries, and in Canada, New Zealand, South Africa, and the UK, commemorative coins were issued.

Jubilee celebrations

In 2002, the Queen celebrated her Golden Jubilee. She marked 50 years on the throne with an extensive tour of the Commonwealth and UK where millions turned out to celebrate during the Jubilee weekend. The highlight was the Party at the Palace, where music stars came together to entertain the crowds at Buckingham Palace.

This year marks the Diamond Jubilee with a host of events and celebrations taking place around the country to celebrate 60 years as Queen of England. Aside from Queen Victoria in 1897, Queen Elizabeth is the only other Monarch to celebrate a Diamond Jubilee.

The Queen, accompanied by the Duke of Edinburgh, received addresses from both Houses of Parliament at Westminster Hall, on 20 March 2012 as part of the Diamond Jubilee celebrations.

Among the guests was current Conservative Prime Minister David Cameron, senior members of the Cabinet and former Labour premiers Tony Blair and Gordon Brown. The Queen reflected on the ancient setting for her address saying it reminded her of "[Britain's] past, and the virtues of resilience, ingenuity and tolerance which created it". She continued, "I have been privileged to witness some of that history and, with the support of my family, rededicate myself to the service of our great country and its people now and in the years to come." ■

Getty Images

JAGUAR LAND ROVER CONGRATULATES HER MAJESTY THE QUEEN

ON THE OCCASION OF HER DIAMOND JUBILEE

Jaguar Land Rover is proud to be a part of the celebrations marking Her Majesty's 60-year reign. Jaguar and Land Rover enjoy a long-standing association with the Royal Household, having been vehicles of choice for Her Majesty and members of the Royal Family from the 1953 Commonwealth Tour through to the 2011 wedding of the Duke and Duchess of Cambridge.

The Jaguar and Land Rover brands are globally recognised and respected for their rich heritage and JLR - a wholly owned subsidiary of India's Tata Motors, a Tata Group company – is acknowledged as one of the world's leading premium automotive businesses.

As the largest manufacturer of premium vehicles in the UK, exporting to more than 170 countries, JLR employs more than 20,000 people in Britain and is a major provider of skilled jobs. Committed to forging deeper relationships with academia and industry suppliers to develop new technologies, JLR is also training the next generation of engineers and designers through its industry-leading apprenticeship and graduate schemes.

With a model portfolio comprising the Land Rover Defender, Freelander and Discovery; the Jaguar XF and XJ saloons and XK sports car; and the Range Rover, Range Rover Sport and newly introduced Range Rover Evoque, JLR continues to be guided by the well-established principles of design and engineering which have brought success for both of the brands and has an absolute focus on producing innovative, relevant and highly desirable vehicles.

We are honoured that this focus has been recognised by our customers throughout our history, none more so than Her Majesty The Queen.

KYRGYZ REPUBLIC

On behalf of the people of Kyrgyzstan and myself, let me express my most sincere congratulations on the momentous day for all British people, the Diamond Jubilee of the 60-year reign of Your Majesty Queen Elizabeth II.

I want to assure Your Majesty that we highly appreciate the existing relations of friendship and cooperation between the Kyrgyz Republic and Great Britain. Confirmation of such a relationship was seen at the opening of the British Embassy in Kyrgyzstan on 8 December this year.

I am confident that with the opening of the British representation in our capital the new horizons of the Kyrgyz and British bilateral cooperation will significantly expand in all mutually acceptable and beneficial areas.

Taking this opportunity, let me wish you, Your Majesty, and your family good health, welfare, happiness; and the friendly British people, peace, happiness and further prosperity.

Almazbek Atambayev

President of the Kyrgyz Republic

MONACO

May I take this opportunity to warmly extend my sincere congratulations to Her Majesty Queen Elizabeth II during the auspicious and historic occasion of her Diamond Jubilee.

The British monarch is an inspiration to millions with her tireless dedication to worthy and charitable causes and the devotion she shows to her many subjects in the Commonwealth and beyond.

For 60 years Her Majesty has worked tirelessly in the interests of the Commonwealth and its people. In an ever-evolving, modern society Her Majesty's stoic and charitable leadership supremely demonstrates the tremendous contribution that sovereign office can bring to so many people.

We are very proud that Her Majesty continues to recognise and support the commitments of HRH Prince Albert and the Principality of Monaco.

Long may she reign.

Her Excellency Mrs Evelyne Genta

Ambassador of the Principality of Monaco

PHILIPPINES

On behalf of the Embassy and the Filipino community in the United Kingdom, I would like to express my most heartfelt congratulations to Her Majesty Queen Elizabeth II on the celebration of the Diamond Jubilee and 60th year of her reign.

For the past 60 years, the Queen has been the manifestation of the true British spirit. Reigning with wisdom and generosity across her kingdom, the Queen has been a genuine inspiration not only to her subjects, but also to the 250,000-strong Filipino community who have been welcomed so warmly into this country.

We look forward to the Queen's continuing success and good health.

Enrique A Manalo

Ambassador of the Republic of the Philippines to the Court of St James's

DENMARK

May I take this opportunity to warmly extend my sincere congratulations to Her Majesty Queen Elizabeth II on the occasion of her Diamond Jubilee.

The British Monarch is an inspiration to millions across the world with her lifelong dedication to worthy and charitable causes. In a modern world, she is a model of both dignity and decorum.

We are honoured that Her Majesty's Armed Forces continue to collaborate closely with the Danish Armed Forces. It is a strong partnership based on common values that has seen the dedicated troops of our two nations work closely together in Afghanistan and Libya in recent years.

We are very proud that Her Majesty Queen Elizabeth II continues to support Her Majesty Queen Margrethe II of Denmark in her role as Colonel-in-Chief of the Princess of Wales's Royal Regiment.

Long may she reign!

Her Excellency Anne Hedensted Steffensen

Ambassador of Denmark

Leading the Legion

Sir John Kiszely's time as national president of The Royal British Legion has already given the Lieutenant General some fond memories, but the best is yet to come ahead of this year's Diamond Jubilee celebrations

When Lieutenant General Sir John Kiszely was asked to extend his tenure as national president of The Royal British Legion by a further 12 months in March of this year, he says he had no hesitation in accepting. Sir John, who will serve an unprecedented four years as the Legion's president, served in the Armed Forces for almost 40 years and had tours of duty in the Falklands – where he was awarded the Military Cross – Northern Ireland, Germany, Cyprus and Iraq. On his retirement from the British Army in 2008, he took over as president from Air Marshal Ian Macfadyen, who recommended him for the post.

about. I enjoy meeting Legion members throughout the country and talking to Legion beneficiaries, as well as the professional staff and the many volunteers – each and every one of them is so important to the charity and makes it what it is today."

Changing image

In Sir John's time as national president, he says he has noticed a marked change in the public perception of the Legion and the work it does on behalf of members of the British Armed Forces. "There has been a real shift in the image of The Royal British Legion over the past two or three years," he believes. "I think a lot of people looked upon the Legion as a charity that took care of World War veterans or that it was exclusive to an older generation – that seemed to be the image that the Legion had. However, it is much more than that – our focus today, as well as looking after older veterans, is very much on the young people who have been involved in campaigns in Iraq and Afghanistan, for example. A lot of our work now revolves around them – not

> ## "Our focus today, as well as looking after older veterans, is on the young people involved in campaigns in Iraq and Afghanistan"

"For me, being national president of The Royal British Legion is a great honour and a huge pleasure," Sir John notes. "Throughout the time I have held the appointment, I have felt hugely honoured whenever I have been working on behalf of such a wonderful charity."

The position of national president is part-time and unpaid. Nevertheless, the honour alone is more than enough for Sir John who, as the figurehead of the charity, has been more than rewarded for his time and efforts by the memories that he will forever have from his time with the Legion. "My role is very much a non-executive position," he says. "However, it has afforded me the opportunity to see a lot of the work that is carried out by the Legion and I have been lucky enough to have met a lot of the people associated with the charity – that is what I really enjoy doing because, after all, people are what the Legion is all

Above, from left: Sir John Kiszely at the Festival of Remembrance, 2010; and at Westminster Abbey Field of Remembrance, 2011

just in terms of welfare but also campaigning and lobbying on their behalf. For example, we were very active last year in persuading the Government to fully honour the principles of the Armed Forces Covenant by enshrining it in law – this is the first time that something like this has ever happened. Also, last November, the Legion helped ensure that the Government did not abolish the post of chief coroner, which we feel is very important for the families of those bereaved."

Awareness of the work of the Legion among the public grows stronger by the year, growing as the sustained conflicts that the British Armed Forces are involved in go on. In turn, the British people have developed a special resonance with the sacrifices that many have made whilst serving, which, says Sir John, is something that the Legion is eternally grateful for. "The British public are, and have always been, wonderfully supportive of our Armed Forces and of The Royal British　>>

"People throughout the world hold our Queen in the highest regard and have tremendous admiration for her"

Clockwise from above left: Her Majesty the Queen opening the Royal British Legion's Haig House, 2009. Sir John Kiszely with the Prime Minister at the Downing Street Poppy Party, 2011; and on Pedal to Paris, 2010

Legion – which is borne out by the overwhelming success of the Poppy Appeal every year. The support of the British people for The Royal British Legion is not only humbling, but also something that we are hugely appreciative of and will certainly never take for granted."

A nation's pride

Building the profile of The Royal British Legion is helped in no small part by the support of Her Majesty the Queen, who, of course, is the charity's patron. With a keen personal interest in the affairs of the Armed Forces, Sir John says Queen Elizabeth II is not only a credit to the Legion, but to the nation and the wider Commonwealth. "From my briefings with the Queen on

the work of the Legion and having met her when she officially opened our new headquarters at Haig House in 2009, I found her to be the most lovable person," he remembers. "What she has done for this country is amazing, not just because monarchy itself is such an important unifying factor and something which is truly great about the UK, but also because, she, herself, is such a wonderful individual. As a nation, it is clear to see that we are so proud of her – people throughout the world hold our Queen in the highest regard and have tremendous admiration for her, which is a source of great pride for the country."

Looking ahead to the Diamond Jubilee celebrations throughout the remainder of 2012, Sir John Kiszely points out that while there will be national highlights broadcast around the world for everyone to enjoy, the most important events for Legion members throughout Britain will be the ones where the Queen visits their own local area. "There is a fantastic programme of activity of Royal visits throughout the country and wherever Her Majesty goes, Legion members will be present. In fact, in many cases Legion members will be meeting the Queen, often for the first time – that will be a most special day for many involved with our charity."

For Sir John himself, the highlight will be the Thames Diamond Jubilee Pageant on Sunday, 3 June, when he will join other members of the Legion on London Bridge to watch the Royal Barge lead the largest flotilla of ships ever assembled. ■

Congratulations to
Her Majesty, Queen Elizabeth II
on her Diamond Jubilee.

It is with the utmost respect, joy and best wishes that CW Publishing congratulates her Majesty Queen Elizabeth II on sixty years on the throne.

Queen Elizabeth II has reigned with poise, elegance, intelligence and open-mindedness; redefining and keeping the Monarchy relevant in an ever changing and challenging Britain.

Her Majesty has not only been an incredibly positive influence on our own country as a symbol of stability and reassurance, but she is also loved across the globe, in particular by the Commonwealth member nations, as shown during her many official royal visits throughout her six decades.

This year, and the month of June in particular, will see a flurry of excited events, celebrations and parties across the nation to celebrate the Diamond Jubilee. 2012 really is a year to rejoice in being British, with the Jubilee and the London Olympics happening to great excitement. Events such as The Big Lunch unite the people of the country by inviting them to arrange street parties and dine together, reminiscent of the street parties of yesteryear.

We thank Her Majesty Queen Elizabeth II for her 60 years as a committed, inspirational Monarch and are eternally grateful for the opportunity to be involved in the Jubilee celebrations in producing this commemorative souvenir for The Royal British Legion; the nation's leading Armed Forces charity, providing welfare, comradeship, representation and Remembrance for serving and ex-Service people, and their families.

On behalf of everyone at CW Publishing may we offer Her Majesty and the Royal Family a wonderful Jubilee year. Long may she reign.

LONDON • NEW YORK
cwpublishinggroup

The work of The Royal British Legion

The Royal British Legion is the nation's leading Armed Forces charity, providing welfare, comradeship, representation and Remembrance for serving and ex-Service people, and their families. Here's how the Legion provides support to those in need

The Royal British Legion was born from a 1921 merger of four charities eager to protect and serve former Servicemen in the wake of World War I. Operating under a Royal Charter, the organisation today is the UK's leading Service charity, with over 360,000 members. It provides practical care, advice and support to serving and ex-Service members of the Armed Forces, veterans of all ages and their families.

Almost nine million Service personnel are eligible for help, and the charity aims to directly help the 500,000 people most in need. Half of the people helped by the charity are below retirement age and, even those who do not receive hands-on help, benefit from the Legion's extensive campaigning work and Remembrance activities.

Back to work

Adjusting to civilian life after a career in the Armed Forces can be very difficult. For this reason, The Royal British Legion has initiated Civvy Street, a website aimed at helping personnel adjust to civilian life and begin a new career. Job vacancies, a CV builder and interview preparation material are available to everyone and, by registering, users can get access to a range of online training courses to help them in their careers. Visit www.civvystreet.org or call free on 0800 169 4073. >>

Widow Amanda Binnie holds a Remembrance cross in memory of her husband Cpl Sean Binnie, acting Sgt, Black Watch, 3rd Battalion, The Royal Regiment of Scotland. Killed in action in Afghanistan, May 2008 (main): Be the Boss beneficiary Derick Sloane (Left)

The Legion made a successful appeal at Tribunal for Afghanistan veteran Aron Shelton in September 2011, restoring his full Disability Living allowance (above). Pop chart stars The Saturdays launch the Poppy Appeal in 2010 (right)

In conjunction with the Legion's partners, the Be the Boss service offers training in setting up small businesses: It helps with writing business plans and assists with financial planning, business 'health checks' and mentoring. The service offers start-up funding of up to £7,500, and further funding to grow businesses after six months. For those that have already been trading for 12 and 24 months, funds of up to £30,000 pounds are available. The Be the Boss programme is accessible at www.civvystreet.org

Lost trails

Friendships are forged during Service, but often comrades can lose contact when they return to their civilian lives. For this reason, The Royal British Legion facilitates Lost Trails, a message board service to help ex-Service men and women locate their former companions. To access it, visit The Royal British Legion website by logging on to www.britishlegion.org.uk

Financial assistance

Since it started in 2007 the Legion's Benefits and Money Advice (BMA) finance service has put £70 million back into people's pockets through increases in benefits, writing off debts and gaining grants. The average beneficiary is approximately £2,800 better off thanks to the Legion's assistance.

The BMA service offers discreet, impartial and non-judgemental advice on finance. The advisors help beneficiaries claim the benefits and tax credits they're entitled to and manage their debts free of charge and in strict confidence. The Legion staff understand the financial difficulties caused by moving regularly, loved ones being away, rejoining civilian life and coping with post-traumatic stress disorder.

Service personnel and families facing unexpected costs can also benefit from the Immediate Needs Grants Scheme, which helps thousands of families every year. The scheme offers essentials for a household in a time of need. Grants can help cover the cost of a funeral, essentials like

Little trooper

When George Taylor saw a news report about a war veteran who was forced to sell war medals to pay a heating and electric bill, he was moved enough to embark on a fundraising career on behalf of The Royal British Legion.

George set up a Never Forget Tribute Fund in the name of his cousin who had served in the Royal Navy before being tragically killed in a motoring accident.

While all fundraising efforts on behalf of The Royal British Legion are admirable and certainly appreciated, what makes George's story all the more remarkable is the fact that he began his campaign when he was just eight years old.

Four years on and he has held tea dances, discos and embarked on gruelling sponsored walks to raise money for the charity. "I really enjoy doing this," George explains. "It has become something of a hobby. I have also had the honour of meeting the Queen at the opening of Haig House in 2010. We had a 20 minute conversation about the work I was doing – she wanted to find out how and why I got involved."

George is determined to carry on his work but he says that none of it would have been possible without his family. "All of my family have helped me," he says "My nan, my mum, my sister and my dad, who thinks he's just a chauffeur. He's certainly not – I couldn't have done any of it without him."

food and clothing, mobility vehicles or adaptations to the family home for a disability and help getting into rented accommodation. As a rule, the charity carefully considers the individual needs in most situations, and encourages people to get in touch.

Home help

Often, just a simple helping hand around the house will do wonders to enhance quality of life. The Royal British Legion has a dedicated, trusted team of experienced people to help carry out low-level maintenance around homes. This includes changing light bulbs and tap washers, putting up shelves, curtain rails and grab rails, fitting smoke alarms and carbon monoxide detectors, fitting and changing door locks and other security features, building access ramps and sheds and installing care phones.

The home improvement service is open to anyone who has served in the Armed Forces for at least seven days (or dependants of someone who has served) and is receiving a means-tested benefit.

>>

The Jockey Club

1750

The Jockey Club congratulations Her Majesty The Queen on the occasion of the 60th Anniversary of Her Accession to the Throne.

We are deeply proud that Her Majesty is our Patron. All involved in British horseracing benefit greatly from her passion for our sport and the support we receive from her.

In celebration of the Diamond Jubilee, we are delighted that our Epsom Downs Racecourse will host Her Majesty and other members of the Royal Family on Investec Derby Day. A few days after her Coronation in 1953, Her Majesty had a runner in The Derby, Aureole, which finished second in a thrilling race. Last year, Her Majesty had another talented three-year-old Thoroughbred, Carlton House, placed third in the famous Classic, in a race that captured the nation's imagination.

The Jockey Club is the largest commercial group in British horseracing and the leading investor and innovator in the UK's second biggest spectator sport. A leader in racing since 1750, today The Jockey Club focuses its resources, influence and assets on ensuring British horseracing remains the best in the world, with all profits returning to the sport.

The Jockey Club owns 14 leading racecourses, including Aintree, home of the John Smith's Grand National; Cheltenham, stage for the prestigious Cheltenham Festival; Epsom Downs, home to the Investec Derby; and Newmarket's Rowley Mile and July Course, considered Flat racing's global HQ.

Other parts of its Group include Jockey Club Estates, its property and land management arm, which operates the famous training grounds at Newmarket and Lambourn; The National Stud, its Thoroughbred breeding, boarding and education arm; and charity, Racing Welfare, which offers help to all racing's people in need.

The Jockey Club is also the largest shareholder in the new QIPCO British Champions Series, which aims to throw the spotlight on the very best races in the UK Flat season and has created a new industry-owned climax at Ascot, QIPCO British Champions Day. It is also the largest shareholder in media company, Racecourse Media Group, which includes satellite TV channel, Racing UK, online service, RacingUK.com and betting shop TV service, TurfTV.

The Jockey Club's vision is for British racing to remain the best in the world for the next 50 years and beyond.

For more information or to go racing, please visit www.thejockeyclub.co.uk

The Jockey Club

1750

THE JOCKEY CLUB CONGRATULATES HER MAJESTY ON THE 60TH ANNIVERSARY OF HER ACCESSION TO THE THRONE

Jockey Club Racecourses

Jockey Club Estates

National Stud

Racing Welfare

www.thejockeyclub.co.uk

Poppy Break Centres

Some Service families may be recovering from an illness, bereavement or other life-affecting events. For this reason, the Legion offers four Poppy Break centres in prime locations around the country. At these locations, it is possible for Service families to unwind from the extraordinary pressures of life in the Armed Forces. The four Poppy Break Centres are Alderson House, Bennet House, Byng House and Somerset Legion House, which cover various catchment areas. Find out more at www.britishlegion.org.uk

For essential repairs the Property Repair Loan Scheme can help. Any charity and serving unit can apply for a grant to support their work if they deliver welfare services to members of the serving and ex-Service community and share the charity's aim of safeguarding the welfare, interests and memory of those who serve or have served in the Armed Forces and their dependants.

Poppy homes

For those with more acute housing needs, The Royal British Legion operates care homes around the country to help current and former Service personnel and their dependants. The charity operates six homes, each providing long-term nursing and personal care, with some also providing dedicated dementia or respite care. The safe, well-equipped homes are designed to feel like a comfortable, genuine home, however long a person stays.

Because the homes are open only to former Service personnel and their dependants, the Poppy Homes system

Above, from left: The Poppy Break Centres offer families an opportunity to relax and unwind. The Royal British Legion offers a home improvement service to beneficiaries. The Personnel Recovery Centres focus on individual needs (right)

fosters a unique camaraderie. This is enhanced by an activity co-ordinator who tailors activities to residents' needs, enabling each person to get involved with group activity sessions, maintain individual hobbies and interests, and develop new ones. The environment is varied, with men and women of different ages and abilities living in the Legion homes, while each home has a Statement of Purpose and Resident Guide to clearly define the care and services provided. Fee levels, which vary depending on the level of care required, can be explained on enquiry, and some people will be able to access financial support for their care from their Local Authority, Social Services or the NHS.

The Legion also works with former Service personnel and their dependants in dire straits: any former Service man or woman (and dependant) who is homeless or living in temporary accommodation is invited to contact the charity for support and practical assistance. The charity is currently working with SSAFA Forces Help on a Prison In-Reach programme to deliver practical help and support

Martin Hunter

"Defence Recovery Capability aims to ensure that wounded, injured and sick Service personnel have support"

for former Service people serving a prison sentence and their dependants.

Defence Recovery Capability

Defence Recovery Capability aims to ensure that wounded, injured and sick Service personnel have the support to help them to recover and either return to Service or make a successful transition to civilian life. A key aspect of this is the Personnel Recovery Centres, a partnership between The Royal British Legion, the Ministry of Defence and Help for Heroes. These facilities aim to help personnel by improving confidence, providing medical care, encouraging physical fitness, focusing on the individual, reskilling and training, and developing life skills through practical projects, activities and outings.

The PRCs are located close to garrisons, giving access to the army's facilities and support, including existing medical, educational and other garrison facilities. They also offer the chance to recover in a military environment. There is no set length of stay at a PRC – everyone recovers at different rates and in different ways, according to their personalised plan.

The Royal British Legion has pledged its largest ever single donation (£50 million) to Defence Recovery Capability. This will be used to fund the operating costs of the four PRCs in the UK and a Personnel Recovery Facility in Germany. It will also help create and operate the Battle Back Centre, which will use adaptive sport and adventurous training to aid recovery.

The sites will be operated by the army but will be open to personnel from all three Services. This is the Legion's most >>

Membership of the Legion is open to anyone who cares about the lives of the Armed Forces family, past, present and future. Members do not all have a Services background, and volunteers are the lifeblood of the charity. The charity offers a range of support and help to Service families, in addition to its campaigning and Remembrance work.

Visit www.britishlegion.org.uk to find out more about the work of the charity and the people it supports.

ambitious endeavour ever, and the largest single project in its 90-year history.

Legal matters

One of the most common ways in which the Legion helps is by guiding personnel and their families through compensation claims, enquiries and inquests. The charity helps claims for illness or injury in Service, as well as the widow, widower, partner or dependant of someone who died as a result of Service in the Armed Forces claim their entitlement, They can also represent those unhappy with a compensation award at an appeal tribunal.

Inquiry and inquest for families bereaved as a result of Service can be daunting, complicated and can cause frustration to already-grieving families. The Independent Inquest Advice service provides the families of those who've died in Service – including reservists on active Service – with free, independent and expert legal advice and assistance. The charity can be with families along the way, providing experienced solicitors' advice at all stages, and referrals to specialist lawyers and other agencies if needed.

Campaigning

In addition to its on-the-ground work, The Royal British Legion has campaigned to further the cause of serving personnel, ex-Service men and women and their families since 1921. Working with politicians, and bringing public pressure to bear, the charity seeks a fairer deal for people who make a substantial sacrifice.

The charity's most recent success, the Leave it Out Ken! Campaign, saw a Government change of heart that allowed a Chief Coroner to be appointed. The post will help

Remembrance events are held each year on 11 November. The Royal British Legion runs a schools programme to educate young people about the importance of Remembrance (above)

bereaved Service families gain more closure on their loss. "The Government's decision to appoint an independent Chief Coroner means that bereaved military families will have the confidence of knowing an impartial judge will provide essential independent leadership to the inquest system, ensuring that its proceedings are thorough, efficient and fair," explains Legion Director General Chris Simpkins.

Remembrance

One of The Royal British Legion's roles is to act as the nation's custodian of Remembrance, ensuring that those who have given their lives for the freedom we enjoy today are never forgotten. During the weeks leading to Remembrance Sunday and Armistice Day, the poppy has become a universal symbol of Remembrance and respect for their sacrifice.

The Legion is committed to helping young people understand the issues of Remembrance, conflict and the importance of peace. To achieve this, the charity offers free learning resources designed to assist teachers and others working with young people. Poppy Travel for Schools and Young People provides tours that help bring the past to life, giving a direct, memorable and moving experience.

The charity operates the UK's year-round centre of Remembrance, the National Memorial Arboretum. This spiritually uplifting place, which honours the fallen, recognises Service and sacrifice, and fosters pride in Britain. With 50,000 maturing trees and 160 memorials, it is a beautiful and lasting tribute to all Service personnel. To find out more about the National Memorial Arboretum, turn to page 35.

PAKISTAN

It is my proud privilege to extend, on behalf of the Government and people of Pakistan, the Pakistani diaspora in the United Kingdom, and on my personal behalf, our warmest felicitations to Her Majesty Queen Elizabeth II on the auspicious occasion of Her Majesty's Diamond Jubilee on the throne and as Head of the Commonwealth. It is indeed a significant milestone in the history of the Commonwealth.

The Commonwealth is a unique organisation that rightly takes pride in its diversity and the fundamental values and principles. Throughout this long journey of six decades, the Queen has remained an inspiring symbol of unity and strength for the Commonwealth. Her generous impression is visible in all the spheres of Commonwealth activities. Under Her Majesty's charismatic leadership, the Commonwealth, while preserving its special character, has also evolved into a dynamic and progressive organisation fully capable of tackling the contemporary and the future challenges.

While we celebrate this historic occasion in 2012, the Commonwealth family owes its wholehearted gratitude to the Queen for her meritorious services towards upholding and promoting the cause of the Commonwealth. The unprecedented celebrations across the Commonwealth to mark the occasion would indeed be a befitting tribute to Her Majesty's innumerable contributions to the Commonwealth.

I would like to extend, on behalf of the Government and people of Pakistan, the Pakistani diaspora in the United Kingdom and on my personal behalf, our most sincere wishes for Her Majesty's health and happiness, and for the continued progress and prosperity of the entire Commonwealth family.

His Excellency Wajid Shamsul Hasan

High Commissioner

PERU

On the occasion of the celebration of Your Majesty's 60th anniversary of accession to the throne, it is my great pleasure to express the most cordial congratulations of the Peruvian people and Government, as well as my own.

On this special opportunity, I would like to express my best wishes for Your Majesty's personal happiness and prosperity for the British people. Likewise, I would also like to reaffirm Peru's interest in further strengthening the traditional ties of friendship between our nations.

I avail myself of this opportunity to present to Your Majesty, the assurances of my highest and most distinguished consideration.

Ollanta Humala Tasso

President of the Republic of Peru

GIBRALTAR

Last year, The Royal British Legion celebrated its 90th Anniversary. In Gibraltar the Branch was first established on the 18th October 1945, shortly after the Second World War, in which we played an important and proud part. Many Gibraltarians had by then become well acquainted with the work of the Legion helping the families of those who gave their lives or were wounded defending the United Kingdom. Every year, millions of pounds are collected on Poppy Day and in Gibraltar, our Branch looks after the families of those who have served in the Royal Gibraltar Regiment.

Gibraltarians are very proud of their allegiance to The Royal British Legion and the commendable work it does in favour of the Crown and past and present members of the Armed Forces. The many Gibraltarian families, including my own, who suffered the blitz in London during the dark days of the Second World War, have always admired and contributed to this noble cause. The defence of freedom and democracy by our Armed Forces requires the work of The Royal British Legion to continue and we must all strive to participate with affection and solidarity towards those who gave everything so that the rest of us could live in peace.

On behalf of the People of Gibraltar, I send our best wishes to The Royal British Legion on this historic and memorable occasion.

Fabian Picardo

Chief MInister of Gibraltar

Tradition, pageantry and continuity are something the City of London Corporation has in common with Her Majesty The Queen.

They are important elements in the way both work. For us these range from the magnificent surroundings of our Guildhall (from where the City is governed) to icons of London like Tower Bridge – one of five Thames bridges we look after – shown here in celebratory fashion and which will be specially lit to highlight the 2012 Games. It also includes the welcome we give to

foreign heads of state on behalf of the Monarch and the government.

While we pride ourselves on our rich heritage, it only underpins the work we carry out. No office of state or organisation can stand still and over the decades both The Queen and the City Corporation have adapted to changing times to ensure we remain relevant and vital to our country.

The City Corporation's history dates back centuries but we have

a modern outlook that matches that of the City we serve. We provide local and policing services for the City – one square mile in the centre of London. These are provided to the highest standard for our 9,000 residents, the third of a million people who work here and the numerous visitors who seek out our special mix of ancient and modern.

Many of our services are unique and reach beyond the Square Mile to benefit London and the nation. Our Barbican Centre,

A long and distinguished history

CITY OF LONDON

Billingsgate, Smithfield and Spitalfields Markets, the Monument, Hampstead Heath, Epping Forest and the Old Bailey are just some examples – many provided from our own resources at no cost to taxpayers. We don't forget our neighbours either. We have been working in partnership for many years to help regenerate surrounding boroughs – from employment, training, advice and skills to available space for small and medium sized businesses. And our City Bridge Trust is London's largest grant-giving charity, supplying grants worth more than £15m each year to vital causes.

Alongside these we have a special remit to support and promote the business City. We work to keep the Square Mile's position as the world leader in international finance and business services which includes the work of our annually elected Lord Mayor – a dedicated worldwide ambassador for the UK. Although some may take the City's lead in this area for granted it has only been during Queen Elizabeth II's reign that it has become the global leader it is today.

Over the years we have welcomed Her Majesty to the City many times, and hope to do so many more times in the future. We have celebrated with others the milestones of her reign – the coronation, silver, golden and now diamond jubilees.

Congratulations to Her Majesty The Queen on Her Diamond Jubilee from the City of London.

SPAIN

To Your Majesty Queen Elizabeth II, on the occasion of the Diamond Jubilee 2012, may I, on behalf of the Kingdom of Spain, convey my deepest congratulations for the outstanding and priceless contribution that, throughout 60 years on the throne, Your Majesty has made both to her country as monarch, as well as to the friendly relations between the United Kingdom and Spain. History already bears witness to Your Majesty's focus and determination which undoubtedly are and will be an example for all.

Carles Casajuana

Ambassador of Spain

NEW ZEALAND

Queen Elizabeth II has been New Zealand's Queen and our Head of State since 6 February 1952. The date is significant in New Zealand history as it was on 6 February 1840, that my predecessor Governor William Hobson signed the Treaty of Waitangi with 40 Māori rangatira (chiefs) in the name of Queen Elizabeth's great-great-grandmother, Queen Victoria. The Treaty established New Zealand as a modern nation.

Her Majesty has visited our shores 10 times as Queen, meeting people from all walks of life and from all parts of the country. She was the first reigning monarch to open the New Zealand Parliament, and made her Christmas broadcast for 1953 from Government House in Auckland. She continues to be held in very high esteem by the people of New Zealand for her dedication to her duties, her work in promoting the work of charities and royal patronages and as Head of the Commonwealth.

Her Majesty has long been a tireless advocate of those serving in the military and remains the Colonel-in-Chief or Captain-General of several New Zealand Army regiments and corps. As Patron of both The Royal British Legion and the Royal New Zealand Returned and Services Association, Queen Elizabeth has been a strong supporter of their work to help and advocate for those who have served, and their families.

As Governor-General and Her Majesty's representative in New Zealand, I send my best regards to members of the Royal British Legion as they mark the Queen's Diamond Jubilee in 2012.

Lt Gen The Rt Hon Sir Jerry Mateparae, GNZM QSO

Governor-General of New Zealand

MEXICO

I am delighted and honoured to express, on behalf of the Government of Mexico, our sincerest congratulations for the celebration of the Diamond Jubilee of Queen Elizabeth II. Since 1952 Her Majesty's leadership has proven to be an eloquent example of the finest qualities that characterise the United Kingdom and all other states that integrate the Commonwealth.

Throughout the past 60 years the world has gone through volatile and rapidly changing circumstances, however the Queen has been unshakeable in her commitment to the principles that her realms subscribe to, such as the promotion of personal liberty and global peace, as well as complete intolerance to any form of racial discrimination.

This core of values – alongside constantly growing relations in multilateral institutions, trade, tourism and education – are yet another bridge that brings Mexico and the United Kingdom increasingly closer and fosters our mutual understanding day by day.

Even though it is true that anniversaries are times to look back at past experiences, they also serve as an occasion to celebrate achievements reaped at present and evaluate the challenges that lie ahead. Taking into consideration the admiration and affection that Her Majesty gives rise to both at home and abroad, it is inevitable and fitting to conclude that her reign has been and will continue to be one of supreme brightness.

I once again take the occasion to convey Mexico's best wishes to Queen Elizabeth II on a year that most rightly honours her exemplary service to her people and reassure Her Majesty of my highest considerations.

Eduardo Medina-Mora

Ambassador of Mexico to the Court of St James's

PANAMA

Her Majesty,

It is our sincerest pleasure to extend our warmest congratulations on the occasion of the Diamond Jubilee anniversary of your 60 years on the throne, serving Great Britain with honour and dignity.

We very much appreciate the positive influence that the United Kingdom has under your reign and we are confident the legacy will have lasting significance in the ever-changing affairs of the world.

Ana Irene Delgado

Ambassador of the Republic of Panama

Plans for the Party

Millions of people are expected to join in the Queen's Diamond Jubilee celebrations. Take a closer look at what to expect this June

As the celebration of the Queen's Diamond Jubilee approaches, event organisers are readying themselves for what promises to be a memorable weekend. A host of large-scale events will be taking place around the country during the extended weekend at the beginning of the month

(2-5 June), including many that the public can organise and play an active role in.

Her Majesty the Queen will begin marking the 60th anniversary of her accession with a trip to the Epsom Derby on Saturday, 2 June, while the celebrations will climax the following Tuesday with the royal procession.

"To hold a Big Lunch requires no specially laid plans, and an event can range from a simple picnic-style get-together to a fully-blown street party"

The events are varied; some are one-off's, such as the BBC concert at Buckingham Palace, and others, like The Big Jubilee Lunch, are annual events that have been given special prominence for 2012.

The Big Lunch

The Big Lunch, an event now in its fourth year, will be held this year on Sunday, 3 June at Buckingham Palace and has officially been included as part of this year's Jubilee Programme. The focus of the lunch is for neighbours all across the country to get to know each other and in doing so, to promote a sense of community and friendship in their area. The Big Lunch encourages all neighbourhoods across the United Kingdom to get involved, offering free starter

Main picture: 'Party at the Palace' was the pop concert held at Buckingham Palace for the Queen's Golden Jubilee in June 2002. The Duchess of Cornwall, Patron of the Big Jubilee Lunch, visits St Peter's School in London, March 2012 (above right)

packs and tips on how to hold their own Big Lunch event. To hold a Big Lunch requires no specially laid plans, and an event can range from a simple picnic-style get-together to a fully-blown street party. As a testament to its past success, the Big Lunch has received sponsorship from well-known brands like Asda, Kingsmill and EDF Energy. The event is also part-funded by the National Lottery.

At past lunches, as many as two million people have turned out to be part of the festivities; however, the organisers of this year's event hope to draw in even more participants. Particularly as some 10 million took part in the Queen's Silver Jubilee celebrations in 1977. Cardiff, which held a street party then to mark the Silver Jubilee, is one of the hundreds of cities and towns to announce a Big Lunch. Cardiff Council says St Mary's Street will be the focal point of the celebrations, with music and food available from 12-7pm.

Getty Images

BBC Concert

The BBC Diamond Jubilee concert will take place on Monday, 4 June, outside Buckingham Palace. The event will see a host of stars from the music industry including Sir Paul McCartney, Sir Elton John and Dame Shirley Bassey take to the stage in celebration of the Queen's Diamond Jubilee.

The event is being jointly organised by the BBC and Take That singer and X Factor judge Gary Barlow, who has said the concert will "transcend multiple decades of music". A crowd of over 10,000 are expected to attend, all of whom will receive free-of-charge tickets through a national ballot where random winners will be chosen. The event will be broadcast to viewers around the world on BBC One and BBC Radio 2, while ABC will beam the event straight into the living rooms of viewers in the United States.

U2, Tom Jones, Cliff Richard, Annie Lennox, Madness, Lang Lang, Jools Holland, Alfie Boe, Jessie J and JLS are among the names that will play at the event, ensuring that there is something for all age groups to enjoy. As the full line-up was announced, BBC One controller Danny Cohen said: "BBC One is honoured to be the broadcast host of this magnificent concert to celebrate the Diamond Jubilee. This will be a music event like no other, with Britain's greatest musical stars performing to celebrate this great occasion." After the concert, the Queen will light the National Beacon as part of the Jubilee Beacon celebration.

Jubilee beacons

To mark the Queen's 60th year as monarch, thousands of beacons will be lit by celebrants across the UK, the Channel Islands and the Isle of Man on Monday, 4 June. The Queen herself will light the National Beacon outside Buckingham Palace directly after the BBC Concert, while beacons will also be seen on top of St James' Palace, the Tower of

> *"The goal of the project is to light 2012 beacons, and will also include contributions from other Commonwealth members"*

London, Killyleagh Castle in Northern Ireland and the Palace of Holyroodhouse in Scotland. The goal of the project is to light 2,012 beacons, and will also include contributions from other Commonwealth members.

Some beacons will be placed in a number of other high-profile locations. Sixty beacons are expected to line Hadrian's Wall, members of the Air Corps will place them at the summit of Pen Y Fan Mountain in Wales, and the tallest school in the UK, Flash Church of England Primary School in Staffordshire, will have 10 pupils place a beacon at the top of the building.

Britain has a long history of marking events with the lighting of beacons. Beacons were present at both the Queen's Silver Jubilee in 1977 and again at her Golden

Jubilee in 2002. Queen Victoria used them to mark her Diamond Jubilee in 1897.

The Thames Diamond Jubilee Pageant

The Thames Diamond Jubilee Pageant will see one of the largest flotillas of ships ever assembled on the Thames sail up the river in celebration of the Diamond Jubilee.

Up to 1000 ships and boats of all shapes and sizes are expected to turn out for the event, which takes place on Sunday, 3 June. Vessels will range from modern-day craft to wooden sail boats and steam-engine ships and barges will come from the UK, the Commonwealth, >>

Main picture: The stage and audience for Party at the Palace, the pop concert held for the Golden Jubilee in 2002. It is expected that 60 beacons will be lit along Hadrian's Wall (above)

Getty Images

and around the world. The Queen will lead the event, taking her place aboard the Royal Barge at the head of the flotilla.

The event is sure to be a noisy occasion with a carnival atmosphere, with many of the ships using bells, whistles and horns to get the attention of the spectators that will line the river banks.

Among the larger ships taking part is a floating bell tower with eight bells, each marked with the name of a member of the Royal Family, and the Gloriana, a rowing vessel powered by 18 oarsmen. The event is not exclusively organised for experienced sailors however, and 30,000 members of the public are expected to take part in the event by boarding hundreds of passenger boats. Several ships that took part in the Dunkirk rescue will also be on show. Contributions from the Armed Forces, police and fire and rescue services will also be among those sailing the 7.5 mile journey.

The event mirrors the celebration to mark Queen Victoria's Jubilee, when she rode 10 miles in a gilded landau through cheering crowds, waving to her subjects.

The Pageant is being organised and coordinated by Lord Salisbury, chairman of the Thames Diamond Jubilee Foundation and Adrian Evans, the pageant master. The Thames Diamond Jubilee Foundation aims to raise funds from the public not only for the Pageant, but for charitable

organisations too. Large contributions are also being made by Michael Lockett CVO, an entrepreneur and philanthropist who has worked on a number of international events, and the Mayor of London, Boris Johnson. The Port of London Authority will be responsible for the safety of the public during the Pageant.

Jubilee Time Capsule

The Jubilee Time Capsule is an online social archive being launched as part of the Queen's Diamond Jubilee celebrations. The project asks for members of the public to put together a collection of images and/or comments from any occasion, personal or public, that took place during the Queen's reign. Entries are being submitted by people from all over the UK; with historians, schools, universities, families, youth organisations among the most eager contributors.

Buckingham Palace has announced that the best of the collection will be chosen by a set of judges and presented to the Queen in a Diamond Collection presentation. Dr Danny Sriskandarajah, director of the Royal Commonwealth Society, an educational society dedicated to encouraging young people to discover their skills, showed his enthusiasm for the project by saying: "We want this to be the best gift the Queen has ever received, a crowd-sourced people's

Getty Images

"The Jubilee Time Capsule is an online social archive being launched as part of the Queen's Diamond Jubilee celebrations"

history of the last 60 years. Anyone, anywhere in the world can share their story and be part of the Diamond Jubilee celebrations." The project is being supported by Capsool, a newly formed messaging company based in Manchester and South Africa.

The procession

Among the central attractions of the Diamond Jubilee celebrations is the procession, which will take place on Tuesday, 5 June.

In an event that shares parallels with the Royal Wedding in April 2011, the Queen and the Duke of Edinburgh will ride through the streets of Westminster in a decorative carriage, followed closely by Prince Charles and the Duchess of Cornwall, Camilla Parker Bowles, the Duke and Duchess of Cambridge, Prince William and Kate Middleton, and Prince Harry. The Royals will greet cheering crowds as they travel down the Mall and along Whitehall.

The Queen and the Duke of Edinburgh will ride in a 1902 state landau, Buckingham Palace has announced, while

the Household Cavalry Mounted Regiment will escort the couple. The King's Troop Royal Horse Artillery will provide a 60-gun salute in tribute to each of the years the Queen has served as monarch. Military bands and more than 1000 street liners from all areas of the Armed Forces will line the Mall in front of spectators.

After the Royals have finished greeting the crowd on the streets, they will acknowledge the attendees from the balcony at Buckingham Palace, where most recently newlyweds Prince William and Kate Middleton showed their appreciation for people who turned out to celebrate their wedding. A flypast by the RAF will add to the entertainment on the day and, as is the tradition, wow spectators and Royals alike.

Before the procession, the Queen and Duke will host a lunch at Westminster Hall with 700 invited guests. Members of charities, social organisations, schools and small business owners from across the UK will be in attendance to enjoy. A Service of Thanksgiving, which will take place at St Paul's Cathedral, will be held before the procession. ▪

From left: Queen Elizabeth II and Prince Philip ride in a carriage procession at the marriage of Prince William and Catherine Middleton, April 2011. A child has her face painted with a Union Jack at a street party in Stepney, East London in 2002. A portrait of Queen Elizabeth II is placed in a window at a Golden Jubilee street party

60 glorious years.
Thank you, Your Majesty,
for all your tireless work.

We think you deserve a bit of quality
time. The sort that only a well-designed
holiday can bring.

Getty Images

The Queen's prime ministers

The Queen has been served by 12 prime ministers. Here we profile the leaders and discover more about their relationship with the Sovereign

Sir Winston Churchill (1951-1955)

The veteran statesman served as Queen Elizabeth's first prime minister, having won the 1951 general election in partnership with the National Liberal party.

Due to a succession of foreign policy challenges, and his advancing years, his time with the Queen was brief: an ongoing war with Malayan rebels and the Mau-Mau rebellion took up much of his time, while a second stroke, largely kept as a private matter, encouraged him to hand over the reins of power to Anthony Eden in 1955.

Nevertheless, the hero of the Second World War was reported to be among the Queen's favourite prime ministers. On his retirement from public life, she offered to make him Duke of London, but this was declined as it would have compromised the political career of his son, Randolph.

She had already conferred a knighthood on Churchill during 1953, in recognition of his services to Britain, and invested him with the insignia of the Order of the Garter. He became the one MP to be elected during the reign of both Queen Elizabeth II and Queen Victoria.

On his death in 1965, the Queen sent a moving message to Lady Churchill. "The whole world is the poorer by the loss of his many-sided genius, while the survival of this country and the sister nations of the Commonwealth, in the face of the greatest danger that has ever threatened them, will be a perpetual memorial to his leadership, his vision, and his indomitable courage," she wrote. The words were matched with action: by royal decree, his body lay in state for three days and a state funeral was held for him at St Paul's Cathedral, which the Queen attended in person. >>

Princess Elizabeth (as was) greeting Winston Churchill at Guildhall, March, 1950

> *"Following in the footsteps of Sir Winston Churchill, Anthony Eden was a popular candidate for the role"*

Anthony Eden (1955-1957)

Following in the footsteps of Sir Winston Churchill, Anthony Eden was a popular candidate for the role of prime minister, thanks to his long wartime service.

After a snap general election in 1955 – which increased the Conservative majority in parliament – he focused primarily on foreign policy, but managed to preside over Britain's smallest-ever recorded unemployment rate.

Eden did not have as much day-to-day contact with Queen Elizabeth II on matters of state as some of his peers: indeed, during the crucial Suez Crisis month of October 1956, the Court Circular recorded just two meetings between the Prime Minister and the Queen. The controversial decision to use Armed Force against Colonel Nasser, and the operation's failure, cast a shadow over his premiership. On 9 January 1957, he resigned due to ill health.

On his resignation, Eden did not proffer advice on who was to be his successor. The Queen consulted Lords Salisbury and Kilmuir for the opinion of the Cabinet, along with Winston Churchill, (following the precedent of George V consulting Salisbury's father and Arthur Balfour upon Andrew Bonar Law's resignation in 1923) and learned that Harold Macmillan was the near-unanimous choice of the Conservative Party. Eden himself was created Earl of Avon in 1961.

Harold Macmillan (1957-1963)

When the Queen invited Harold Macmillan to form an administration following Anthony Eden's sudden departure, he warned that his Government would probably not last six weeks. However, he steered Great Britain successfully for over six years – as Queen Elizabeth pointed out during their final audience in October 1963.

Arguably the high point of a successful premiership was his 1959 election victory, in which he famously remarked that "most of our people have never had it so good". It summed up the optimism of an age: the average real pay for industrial workers had risen by over 20 per cent since 1951,

Britain was withdrawing from its empire in neater fashion than in previous years, and the special relationship with the United States was healing after Suez. He also became the first British prime minister to visit the Soviet Union, and actively encouraged a 'thaw' in the Cold War.

In his dealings with the Queen, Macmillan was supportive of her desire to ensure descendants not eligible for a royal title would be known by the surname Mountbatten-Windsor. He also helped in the diplomatic shuffling when a state visit to Ghana was cancelled due to her pregnancy.

Despite major success with the 1963 Partial Test Ban Treaty and the creation of European Free Trade Association (EFTA), his Government was damaged by the Profumo affair of 1963. That year, he was taken ill on the eve of the Conservative Party conference, and incorrectly diagnosed with inoperable prostate cancer. Resigning in October 1963, he nominated Foreign Secretary Alec Douglas-Home as successor, but declined a peerage. Macmillan accepted the distinction of the Order of Merit from the Queen in 1976. He remained active in political discourse until his death in 1986, and his public memorial service in Westminster Abbey was attended by the Queen. Harold Macmillan was nicknamed 'Supermac' during his earlier political career for his pragmatism, wit and unflappability.   >>

(Left): The Queen shakes hands with Conservative Prime Minister, Anthony Eden, 1956. (Above): Queen Elizabeth II visits Harold Macmillan, Edinburgh, 1960

Sir Alec Douglas-Home (1963-1964)

Sir Alec Douglas-Home served as Prime Minister from October 1963 to October 1964, succeeding Harold Macmillan.

Douglas-Home was appointed prime minister at the request of Macmillan, despite not being a member of the House of Commons at the time. In order to become eligible for the position, Douglas-Home gave up his peerage and successfully contested a by-election in order to regain his seat. He had assumed his seat in the House of Lords, giving up his seat in the Commons, after his father, the Earl of Home, passed away in 1951.

After his term as prime minister ended in 1964, Douglas-Home served as leader of the opposition for nine months before being replaced as party leader by Edward Heath.

He returned to Government later as Foreign Secretary after the Conservatives won the 1974 general election under Heath, and remains the only former prime minister to take up a position in someone else's cabinet. He was awarded a knighthood during his time as Foreign Secretary. Douglas-Home retired following a Labour victory in the 1974 election.

Harold Wilson (1964-1970 & 1974-1976)

Harold Wilson began his first term as prime minister in March 1964 after an election victory over Sir Alec Douglas-Home's Conservative Party.

In all, Wilson won four general elections as Labour Party leader, serving for a total of eight years. His first term saw a number of important pieces of social legislation pass through the Commons, including some that softened the law's stances on immigration, divorce, homosexuality, abortion and censorship. Wilson's time in office also saw the abolition of capital punishment in the UK and the winding down of wartime rations.

He guided Labour to a resounding 96-seat majority in the general election of 1966. During this term, Wilson applied for UK entry into the EEC for a second time – the first attempt was vetoed by Charles DeGaulle in 1963. The UK's eventual acceptance, in 1973, was negotiated by Sir Edward Heath, who served as prime minister between Wilson's two terms.

After his return to office in 1974, Wilson led a minority Labour government, after failing to form a coalition with the Liberals. From Downing Street, Wilson rolled out more liberal reforms, the most significant of which was a record 25 per cent increase in state pensions. Wilson also introduced

Getty Images

> ## "The Queen attended a meal to mark Wilson's resignation. The only other PM she had visited personally was Churchill"

further food and housing subsidies, and set aside an extra £2 billion for benefit payments. After serving two years, Wilson resigned at the age of 60, citing physical and mental exhaustion.

As a sign of gratitude to Wilson, the Queen attended a meal at Downing Street to mark his resignation. The only other prime minister she had visited personally was Winston Churchill.

Sir Edward Heath (1970-1974)

Edward Heath assumed office after defeating the Labour Party, led by Harold Wilson, in the 1970 general election.

Before becoming prime minister, Heath had been President of the Board of Trade under Sir Alec Douglas-Home and Secretary of State for Industry, Trade and Regional Development. He had also served in the Second World War, receiving several medals for his service, and was Shadow Chancellor prior to the election in 1970.

Heath's term in office saw the decimalisation of sterling, the UK's ascension into the EEC and the introduction of

several social policies. Heath introduced benefits for the disabled, widows' benefits and an allowance for those caring for elderly relatives. State pensions were introduced for those aged 80 and over, the Social Security Act was passed and Children's Allowance was raised. The age a student could leave school was also raised, to 16.

In 1972, he introduced the Local Government Act, which saw the creation of so-called metropolitan counties, although these titles did not carry any relevance until Prime Minister John Major created the 10 Government Office Regions.

Heath left office in 1974, having failed to negotiate an agreement on a coalition with the Liberals after the 1974 election, leaving Labour to rule as a minority government. He was replaced as leader of the party the following year after being defeated by his Science Secretary, Margaret Thatcher in a leadership contest.

He ended his political career in June 2001, having served as Father of the House since 1992. The longest serving MP, he was knighted after his resignation.

Conservative Prime Minister Alec Douglas-Home, 1961 (far left). The Queen and Prince Philip listening to an address by Harold Wilson, September 1975 (above left). Prime Minister Edward Heath addresses the Conservative Party press conference shortly before the General Election, 1974 (above)

>>

James Callaghan (1976-1979)

James Callaghan began his term as prime minister after Harold Wilson's surprise resignation in 1976.

During his time in office Callaghan introduced the Police Act 1976, which provided for the establishment of an independent Police Complaints Board, the Rent (Agricultural) Act, which provided security of tenure for farm workers' residence, and the Housing Act 1977, which placed the responsibility for housing the homeless on local authorities.

As prime minister of a minority government, Callaghan often negotiated with opposition parties in order to get bills through, including establishing the Lib-Lab pact, a working relationship agreement with the Liberals, that would see some of the party provide its support to Labour.

Callaghan also presided over the Winter of Discontent, which in 1978-79, saw the country stalled by several strikes and arguments over pay. Pre-Winter polls had Labour with a comfortable lead over the Conservative Party; however, on the other side of the Winter, the Tories' lead often exceeded 20 points.

Callaghan's government was defeated in a vote of confidence in the House of Commons by one vote, 311-310. Callaghan was succeeded as prime minister by Margaret Thatcher. He is the only person to have served in all four major Government posts: prime minister, chancellor, home secretary and foreign secretary and was given a knighthood by the Queen on his retirement in 1987. Callaghan died at the age of 93 on 26 March 2005.   >>

Labour politician and later Prime Minister, James Callaghan at the 73rd annual party conference, Westminster, London

"Callaghan is the only person to have served in all four major Government posts, including prime minister and chancellor"

Getty Images

Investec Asset Management warmly congratulates Her Majesty the Queen on the celebration of her Diamond Jubilee

Investec Asset Management is proud to support The Royal British Legion.
Our experienced investment teams and international perspective allow us
to offer diverse investment solutions, from fixed income to global equities,
frontier markets and commodities and resources.

For more information, please visit **www.investecassetmanagement.com**

The value of investments can fall as well as rise and you may get back less
than you invested.

Out of the Ordinary™

Getty Images

Margaret Thatcher (1979-1990)

When the Conservatives came to power in 1979, Margaret Thatcher, as leader of the party became Britain's first female prime minister. Her core policies involved privatisation of state utilities, union reform, reduced taxation and cuts to social expenditure. This strategy, known as Thatcherism, divided opinion; she was hero to some and villain to others.

Victory in the Falklands War in 1982 improved her popularity greatly and led to a landslide re-election. Throughout her tenure, she had a strong relationship with US President Ronald Reagan with whom she shared a common belief in the benefits of *laissez faire* economics as well as a mutual mistrust of Soviet communism. Thatcher was also staunchly against European Union interference in UK political matters.

> *"In 1987 the Queen amended the Order of the Garter to include women. In 1995 the Queen bestowed the honour on Margaret Thatcher"*

In 1987 Thatcher won an unprecedented third term as prime minister. However, policies such as the Poll Tax (essentially a tax per head rather than a tax based on a percentage of income) led to public unrest and a swift decline in her popularity. In November 1990, Michael Heseltine challenged Thatcher's position as head of the party and, when John Major emerged victorious in the ballot, Thatcher resigned from the party. Today, her legacy still divides opinion – she is credited in some quarters with jumpstarting the UK economy and lowering inflation, while others blame her for a rise in unemployment and a widening of the rich-poor divide.

A great deal has been written about the relationship between Mrs Thatcher and the Queen but much is dismissed as unfounded conjecture. Lady Thatcher and the Queen certainly had contrasting personalities – Thatcher's forceful and authoritative manner contrasted with the Queen's generally soft and reserved approach. Sources have claimed that the pair clashed over Thatcherite policies and Commonwealth sanctions against apartheid

Queen Elizabeth II and Margaret Thatcher at the former prime minister's 70th birthday party, London, 1995

South Africa. However, Tim Bell, Thatcher's former advisor dismissed reports that the pair disliked each other, stating, "Margaret has the deepest respect for the Queen and all her family". Thatcher herself rubbished rumours of a rift, asserting, "I always found the Queen's attitude towards the work of the Government absolutely correct (...) stories of clashes between 'two powerful women' were just too good not to make up".

In 1987, Queen Elizabeth II amended the statutes of Order of the Garter (the highest order of knighthood in England) to include 'Lady Companions of the Order'. In 1995, the Queen bestowed the honour on Margaret Thatcher.   >>

Proud to celebrate your Coronation
in 1953 and just as proud to
celebrate your Diamond Jubilee
Lloyds Bank Regent Street branch, decorated
to celebrate the coronation in 1953

HAPPY AND GLORIOUS

From our Chairman, Sir Winfried Bischoff,
and everyone at Lloyds Banking Group, sincere
congratulations on your Diamond Jubilee.

**LLOYDS
BANKING
GROUP**

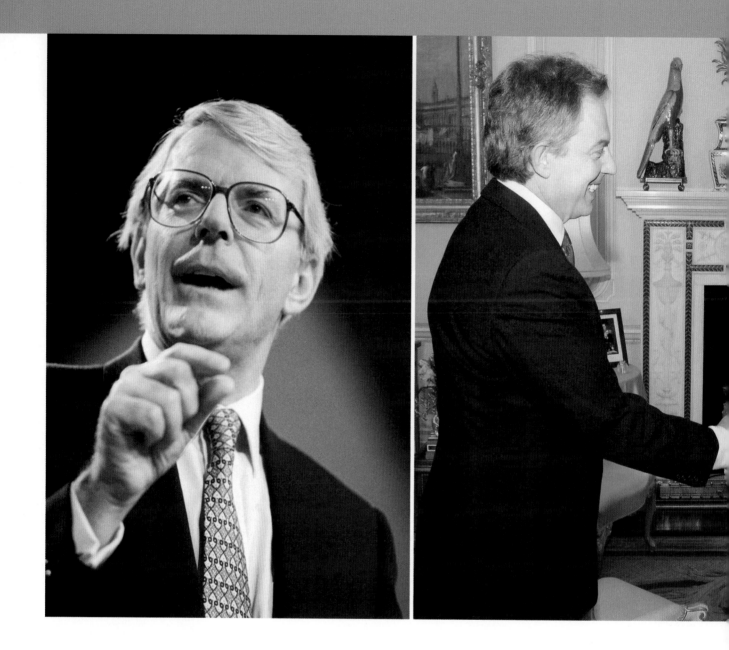

Sir John Major (1990-1997)

John Major took over as prime minister and leader of the Conservatives, after emerging victorious from a challenge to Margaret Thatcher's leadership in 1990. His first action as prime minister was to oversee the UK's involvement in the Gulf War. Major secured Britain's right to opt out of a European single currency at the Maastricht Treaty in 1991, calling the amended treaty a "game, set and match for Britain".

One of his greatest successes was his involvement in bringing about an IRA ceasefire in 1994 and laying the foundations for the Good Friday Agreement. Major revealed that the Troubles were one of the key matters discussed in his weekly meetings with the Queen, stating that "the Queen approved" of attempts to solve the conflict in Ireland. Major and the Conservatives lost power to the Labour Party in 1997.

John Major spoke out in support of the weekly conferences with the Queen. "The Queen as a Head of State has a right to know what is happening," he said. Major was also impressed by Her Majesty's knowledge and openness to differing points of view. "The Queen's a wise lady. She understands different views – she has never been perturbed by people who've had different views to her. She understands them."

Tony Blair (1997-2007)

Tony Blair became Prime Minister after leading Labour to landslide victory over the Conservative Party in 1997. Blair's New Labour involved a move away from state socialism to a model of 'ethical socialism' (capitalism with a focus on social justice). Blair is the Labour Party's longest-serving prime minister, remaining in power for three consecutive terms.

In 1997, he oversaw the creation of devolved institutions in Scotland, resulting in the establishment of a Scottish parliament. The creation of the Welsh Assembly and a devolved parliament in Scotland, as well as substantial progression in Northern Ireland, were some of Blair's chief contributions as prime minister. He is widely praised for his contributions to the Northern Irish peace process, which culminated

Gordon Brown (2007-2010)

Gordon Brown served as prime minister for three years after taking over the Labour leadership from Tony Blair. Originally tipped as John Smith's successor as party leader, it was another 10 years before Brown, who served as Chancellor for the period in between, became prime minister. During Labour's 13 years in power, Brown was one of only three members of cabinet to remain in the Government for the full stretch, the others being Jack Straw and Alistair Darling.

During his time in office, Brown continued to implement New Labour's trademark social policies, including introducing The Autism Act 2009, The Child Poverty Act 2010, and The Agency Workers Regulations 2010. He also introduced free cancer medication prescriptions and the Health in Pregnancy Grant to take the financial pressure off expecting mothers.

On his departure from Downing Street, Brown was invited by the Queen to bring his wife and two young sons, John and Fraser, with him to Buckingham Palace as he handed in his resignation. This was the first time the Queen invited an outgoing prime minister to bring their family to the Palace. Media reports suggested that the Queen made the decision to invite the family after being touched by pictures of the young boys leaving Downing Street. >>

"On his departure from Downing Street, Brown was invited by the Queen to bring his wife and two sons with him to Buckingham Palace"

in the signing of the monumental Good Friday Agreement in 1998.

Blair led Britain during a turbulent 10 years, which included the 2001 attacks on the World Trade Center's twin towers in New York and the 2005 London underground bombings. After the World Trade Center attacks Blair formed a coalition with George W Bush to mount a "global war on terror'". This involved sending British troops into Afghanistan in 2001 and Iraq in 2003, a decision which was later heavily criticised. In June 2007, Blair was succeeded as prime minister and as leader of the Labour Party by Gordon Brown.

By most accounts the Queen and Tony Blair had a strained relationship yet Blair did show an admiration for the Queen when responding to fears from certain quarters about a move to a single currency. "I know exactly what the British people feel when they see the Queen's head on a £10 note. I feel it too," he said.

Former Prime Minister John Major speaks at the Conservative conference, Blackpool, 1997 (above left). Her Majesty congratulates Tony Blair on winning a third term in Government, 2005 (above)

Getty Images

The Howard de Walden Estate would like to congratulate Her Majesty the Queen on her Diamond Jubilee.

The Howard de Walden Estate owns, manages and leases approximately 92 acres of real estate in Marylebone, London W1. The area is a highly sought after, quiet and distinctive oasis within the heart of central London.

THE HOWARD de WALDEN ESTATE

To find out more about the Estate please visit: www.hdwe.co.uk

Getty Images

David Cameron (2010 to present)

After winning his first term as an MP in 2001, David Cameron rose quickly through the Conservative Party ranks to become leader just four years later, succeeding Michael Howard. He led the party to victory in the 2010 general election at just 43 years of age, becoming the youngest prime minister in almost 200 years.

Despite defeating Labour in the general election, the Conservative Party did not have enough seats to rule with a majority. In order to achieve his aim of forming a government, Cameron invited the Liberal Democrats, led by

Nick Clegg, to help him reach his target. The unprecedented partnership left the coalition with a majority of 76 seats in the House of Commons, with Cameron saying that the parties had managed to put their differences aside to work in the national interest.

Enjoying a good relationship with the Queen, Cameron recently commented on Her Majesty's upcoming Diamond Jubilee in February by thanking her for 60 years of "magnificent service". The Queen, he remarked, rules with "experience, dignity and quiet authority". He is overseeing the huge programme of events this summer as PM. ■

The Queen and Prime Minister David Cameron at 10 Downing Street, London, 2011

ROMANIA

Your Majesty,

I feel myself deeply honoured and privileged for the opportunity to present my heartfelt congratulations marking Your Majesty's Diamond Jubilee 2012.

I would like to express my profound sense of admiration and respect for Your Majesty's fascinating personality, visionary wisdom and dedication for the welfare of the British people during the 60 remarkable years on the throne.

During Your Majesty's reign, Romania and the United Kingdom have built a strong and reliable partnership, witnessing the commitment of the two countries towards an ever-closer fruitful co-operation as members of the European Union and NATO, sharing common values and interests.

On this very special occasion, I would like to convey to Your Majesty the assurances of my highest consideration and best wishes for the years to come.

Dr Ion Jinga

Ambassador of Romania

MALTA

On the occasion of the Diamond Jubilee of Her Majesty Queen Elizabeth II, it is my honour to express my most heartfelt congratulations, as well as those of the Government and people of Malta.

The people of Malta cherish fond memories of Her Majesty as a young naval bride residing in their country before Her accession to the throne and of the visits she later made to Malta as Queen and Head of the Commonwealth. She is held in very high esteem by the Maltese.

Her Majesty is justly renowned for her unflinching dedication to duty and enjoys worldwide approval.

I am pleased to wish Her Majesty many more years of health and service to her nation.

His Excellency Dr George Abela

President of Malta

UNITED KINGDOM

With love and unbounded admiration.

Dame Judi Dench, CH, DBE

UNITED KINGDOM

It is my pleasure and honour to add a personal note of congratulations to the amazing job that the Royal British Legion do.

I can only wish you every success in the astounding role you play within our society and the continuing inspirational message you deliver.

Sir Steve Redgrave, CBE

UNITED KINGDOM

When Queen Elizabeth II became Queen, she said she would be dedicated to the country; she has not let us down, she has continued to shine ever since.

Sir Paul Smith, CBE

UNITED KINGDOM

Congratulations to Her Majesty Queen Elizabeth II on the occasion of her Diamond Jubilee. During her time on the throne, Britain has become a byword for tolerance, multiculturalism and creativity, leading to a true Renaissance of music, literature, painting, architecture and, of course, the culinary arts.

Long may she reign!

Heston Blumenthal, OBE

ROYALS ON TOUR

As part of the Diamond Jubilee celebrations the Royals are paying visits to Commonwealth countries. Discover who is going where and why the Commonwealth is still so important to the monarchy

Head of the Commonwealth

It's not only us Brits who are celebrating 60 years of the Queen's reign. Across the globe people are joining in with the rejoicing of the Diamond Jubilee. And no more so than in the countries of the Commonwealth, of which Her Majesty has been head for the past six decades.

The importance of the role of Head of the Commonwealth cannot be underestimated. It symbolises

and reinforces the links by which the Commonwealth joins people together from around the world. In a world that seems to be getting smaller, due to technological advances, here is a traditional unity born from the past that still exists and is treasured by the Queen and the rest of the Royal Family in Britain. It is a focal part of the work of the monarchy as it exists today.

Getty Images

Strengthening bonds

One of the ways of strengthening these connections is through regular Commonwealth visits. During her reign, the Queen has visited every country in the Commonwealth (with the exception of Cameroon, which joined in 1995 and Rwanda which joined in 2009) and made many repeat visits. One third of the Queen's total overseas visits are to Commonwealth countries. And even in her later years she is still actively travelling abroad to visit the countries as often as possible. The Duke of Edinburgh, The Prince of Wales and other members of the Royal Family are also regular visitors to the Commonwealth.   >>

Main: Queen Elizabeth II talks with the Very Reverend Dr John after attending the annual Commonwealth Day Observance Service, March 2012.
The Queen on her 16th visit to Australia (top).
Duke and Duchess of Cambridge in Calgary, Canada, 2011 (above)

The Queen's Speech

The Queen delivers a message on Commonwealth Day (the second Monday of March). Here are excerpts from the 2012 message:

"One of the great benefits of today's technology-based world is the range of opportunities it offers to understand and appreciate how others live: we can see, hear and enter into the experience of people in communities and circumstances far removed from our own.

Our circumstances and surroundings may vary enormously, for example in the food we eat and the clothes we wear, but we share one humanity, and this draws us all together. The joys of celebration and sympathy of sadness may be expressed differently but they are felt in the same way the world over.

How we express our identities reveals both a rich diversity and many common threads. Through the creative genius of artists – whether they be writers, actors, film-makers, dancers or musicians – we can see both the range of our cultures and the elements of our shared humanity.

'Connecting Cultures', our Commonwealth theme this year, encourages us to consider the special opportunities we have, as members of this unique gathering of nations, to celebrate an extraordinary cultural tapestry that reflects our many individual and collective identities. The Commonwealth treasures and respects this wealth of diversity.

Connecting Cultures is more, however, than observing others and the ways in which they express themselves. This year, our Commonwealth focus seeks to explore how we can share and strengthen the bond of Commonwealth citizenship we already enjoy by using our cultural connections to help bring us even closer together, as family and friends across the globe."

"Prince Harry will visit a number of exotic locations, including Jamaica, Belize and the Bahamas"

Usually during a Commonwealth visit the Queen, or whichever member of the Royal Family is attending, will meet with the prime minister, president or king of that country and have a formal reception and dinner, to welcome them to the country. Often an extensive programme of events and visits will take place after that. The visits are an opportunity to showcase the country's cultural, sporting and business pursuits and successes. It puts that country in the spotlight because images of the royal visit will undoubtedly make it into the world's press. Often, there will be a concert showing the dance, music and arts of the country; a celebration of all that it is to be part of that culture. In that way, it is evidence that the Commonwealth celebrates differences of cultural enrichment, and encourages unity and understanding across the world.

The Jubilee tour

The Queen's Diamond Jubilee will be marked with a series of visits to Commonwealth countries undertaken by members of the Royal Family in support of Her Majesty. Every Realm, of which there are 16, will be visited, as well as other Commonwealth countries, Crown Dependencies and British Overseas Territories. All of the Royal Family are involved. Prince Charles, who is no stranger to royal visits to the Commonwealth, will be accompanied by the Duchess of Cornwall to Australia, Canada, New Zealand, Papua New Guinea, the Channel Islands and the Isle of Man. Some might say the most popular of the young Royals at present, The Duke and Duchess of Cambridge and Prince Harry, will visit a number of exotic locations, including Malaysia, the Solomon Islands, Belize and the Bahamas. Other Royals involved include The Princess Royal, The

Around the Commonwealth

Her Majesty has asked that the 2012 Diamond Jubilee Royal visits include the following:

The Prince of Wales and The Duchess of Cornwall: Australia, Canada, New Zealand, Papua New Guinea, Channel Islands, Isle of Man;

The Duke and Duchess of Cambridge: Malaysia, Singapore, Solomon Islands, Tuvalu;

Prince Harry: Belize, Jamaica, the Bahamas;

The Duke of York: India;

The Earl and Countess of Wessex: Antigua and Barbuda, Barbados, Gibraltar, Grenada, Montserrat, St Kitts and Nevis, St Lucia, St Vincent and the Grenadines, Trinidad and Tobago;

The Princess Royal: Mozambique, Zambia;

The Duke of Gloucester: British Virgin Islands, Malta;

The Duke of Kent: Falkland Islands, Uganda.

Duke of York, The Earl and Countess of Wessex, The Duke of Gloucester and the Duke of Kent. For a full list of which Royals are visiting which countries see the *Around the Commonwealth* box (right).

The Commonwealth Secretariat

The Queen keeps in touch with Commonwealth developments through regular contact with the Commonwealth Secretary-General and his Secretariat. The Secretary-General at present is Kamalesh Sharma. Mr Kamalesh Sharma, an Indian diplomat, became Commonwealth Secretary-General on 1 April 2008. He was appointed to the post by Commonwealth Heads of Government at their meeting in Kampala, Uganda, in November 2007. He previously served as India's High Commissioner to the United Kingdom, where he was closely involved in Commonwealth activities. He was also a member of the Board of Governors of the Commonwealth Secretariat and the Commonwealth Foundation.

Prince Harry tours Jamaica to mark Queen Elizabeth II's Diamond Jubilee (above left). The Duchess of Cornwall and the Prince of Wales address the opening ceremony of New Delhi's XIX Commonwealth Games, 2010 (above)

Based at Marlborough House in London, the Commonwealth Secretariat co-ordinates many Commonwealth activities. Her Majesty also has regular meetings with Heads of Government from Commonwealth countries.

Connecting cultures

The Commonwealth Secretariat oversees Commonwealth Day and Commonwealth Week, which take place in March of each year. This year its theme is 'Connecting Cultures', and focusses not only on connecting global cultures, but within the country that we live in; as we embrace so many immigrants and so many different cultures make up the face of Britain today.

The Commonwealth unites 54 countries with diverse cultures around shared values and vision. Connecting Cultures celebrated a global community of over two billion people of differing beliefs and traditions, with cultural expression a vibrant means of identity and exchange. The Queen attended a reception in London and a variety of events happened around the country and the Commonwealth to mark the week. To support this theme, a special song was composed for the Commonwealth called *Stronger as One*.

THE ENERGY SAVING TRUST ARE VERY PLEASED TO WISH HER MAJESTY THE QUEEN MANY CONGRATULATIONS ON HER DIAMOND JUBILEE

Energy saving advice for you and your lifestyle
www.energysavingtrust.org.uk

 ## UNITED KINGDOM

Congratulations to Her Majesty for 60 years of incredible devotion and dedication to this country and its people. Thank you on behalf of us all and may you long continue.

Sir Michael Caine, CBE

 ## UNITED KINGDOM

Your Majesty,

It's an honour to offer sincere congratulations on the celebration of your Diamond Jubilee and I wish you every success for future continuation of the inspiring work you do.

As head of our state, the moral standard you set and devotion to your duties invokes pride and admiration throughout your country and its loyal subjects.

Long may you reign.

Sir Ian Botham OBE

 ## UNITED KINGDOM

Your Majesty,

May I, amongst countless millions of your subjects, offer you my most sincere congratulations on your coming Jubilee. You are an inspiration to us all.

With humble duty,

Sir Christopher Lee, CBE

 ## UNITED KINGDOM

Your Majesty,

Kristina joins me in offering heartfelt congratulations on the occasion of your Diamond Jubilee. I am proud to serve as one of your Knight Commanders, and give thanks for your continued guidance, wisdom and dedication to our great country.

Sir Roger Moore, KBE, CBE

Serving the nation and its people

The Royal Family has a long-standing tradition of bravery and service in the military and that dedication to serving the country continues today

Prince William, Duke of Cambridge

RANK: Flight Lieutenant, Captain, Lieutenant;

BRANCH OF SERVICE: Royal Air Force, British Army Royal Navy;

UNIT: Blues and Royals, No. 22 Squadron, RAF Search and Rescue Force;

MILITARY TRAINING: Royal Military Academy Sandhurst;

YEARS OF SERVICE: 2006 – present;

MEDALS: Queen Elizabeth II Golden Jubilee Medal.

Prince William, Duke of Cambridge, has served in the Armed Forces since 2006. He was commissioned as a Lieutenant in the Blues and Royals regiment of the Household Cavalry, serving for a short time with his brother, Prince Harry. Two years later, he earned his 'wings' by completing pilot training at the Royal Air Force College Cranwell. In 2009, Prince William was promoted to Flight Lieutenant and underwent helicopter flight training in order to become a full-time pilot with the Search and Rescue Force.

In 2010, he completed his general and special-to-type helicopter training and went on to RAF Valley, performing co-pilot duties on board a Sea King search and rescue helicopter.

At present, Prince William is serving a six-week rotation as a search-and-rescue pilot in the British Falkland Islands. Prince Andrew, Duke of York, also served there as a combat pilot during the Falklands War.

Prince Henry (Harry) of Wales

RANK: Lieutenant, Captain;

BRANCH OF SERVICE: British Army;

WAR SERVICE: Afghanistan;

UNIT: Blues and Royals, Household Cavalry, 1st Mechanised Brigade of the 3rd Mechanised Division;

MILITARY TRAINING: Royal Military Academy Sandhurst

YEARS OF SERVICE: 2005 – present;

MEDALS: Operational Service Medal for Afghanistan, Queen Elizabeth II Golden Jubilee Medal.

Getty Images

"*In 2007 Prince Harry was deployed to Iraq and he later went on to serve 77 days on the frontline of the Afghan War*"

Prince Harry decided to forgo a university education in favour of enrolling in the military. He entered the Royal Military Academy Sandhurst in 2005, where he was known as Officer Cadet Wales. Within a year, he had completed his officer's training and was commissioned as a Cornet in the Blues and Royals – a regiment of the Household Cavalry in the British Army. He was promoted to the rank of Lieutenant in 2008.

The British Ministry of Defence and Clarence House made a joint announcement in February 2007 that Prince Harry would be deployed to Iraq to serve as part of the 1st Mechanised Brigade of the 3rd Mechanised Division. This

decision was fully supported by Harry and he went on to serve 77 days on the frontline in the Afghan War.

In 2008, Prince Harry announced he would follow in the footsteps of his brother and father, and fly military helicopters. He passed his flying assessment at the Army Air Corps Base (AAC) and his father, Prince Charles presented him with his flying wings in 2010. A year later, he was awarded his Apache flying badge and was promoted to the Army rank of Captain.

Prince Harry may well return to Afghanistan again before the withdrawal of British Armed Forces in 2015. >>

Princes William and Harry at Defence Helicopter Flying School, June, 2009. William trained to become an RAF search-and-rescue pilot, and Harry a pilot with the British Army Air Corps

Prince Andrew, Duke of York

RANK: Captain, Helicopter Pilot;

BRANCH OF SERVICE: Royal Air Force, Royal Navy;

WAR SERVICE: The Falklands War;

UNIT: 815 Naval Air Squadron;

YEARS OF SERVICE: 1980-2001;

MILITARY TRAINING: Royal Naval College Dartmouth;

MEDALS: South Atlantic Medal with Rosette.

Prince Andrew, Duke of York, is Commander and Rear Admiral in the Royal Navy in which he served as an active duty helicopter pilot and later instructor in helicopter flight. He saw active service during the Falklands War, flying on multiple missions.

In 1979, Prince Andrew was enrolled at the Royal Naval College Flight, where he trained as a helicopter pilot. He then entered the Royal Naval College Dartmouth. On completion of his training at Dartmouth, he went on to elementary flying training with the Royal Air Force, and later, basic flying training with the Navy at HMS Seahawk.

After being awarded his wings, he moved onto more advanced training and joined his first frontline unit – 820 Naval Air Squadron – serving aboard the HMS Invincible aircraft carrier.

When Argentina invaded the Falkland Islands on 2 April 1982, the HMS Invincible played a major role in the Royal Navy's taskforce charged with retaking control of the islands. Despite concerns for his safety, Prince Andrew remained on board to serve as a Sea King helicopter co-pilot, flying on missions that included anti-submarine and anti-surface warfare. He witnessed the Argentinean attack on the SS Atlantic Conveyor, and was one of the first to help survivors. Described as an excellent pilot and a very promising officer, Prince Andrew was decorated for his service in the Falklands.

He later transferred to RNAS Portland, was trained to fly the Lynx helicopter, and was promoted to the rank of Lieutenant in 1984. He went on to serve aboard HMS Brazen as a flight pilot until 1986, and was deployed to the Mediterranean Sea.

In 1986, he transferred to the General List and served as a helicopter warfare officer in 702 Naval Air Squadron, RNAS Portland, as well as on HMS Edinburgh as an Officer of the Watch and Assistant Navigating Officer. He spent six months deployed in the Far East.

"Described as an excellent pilot and a promising officer, Prince Andrew was decorated for service in the Falklands"

The Duke of York passed the squadron command examination in 1991 and the following year, he completed the Army Staff course, becoming a Lieutenant-Commander. From 1995-96, he was posted as Senior Pilot of 815 Naval Air Squadron – then the largest flying unit in the fleet air arm.

In 2001, he finished his active naval career at the British Ministry of Defence as an Officer of the Diplomatic Directorate of the Naval Staff. Later that year, he retired from the active list of the Navy, and, three years later, was made an Honorary Captain. In 2010, on his 50th birthday, he was promoted to Honorary Rear Admiral.   >>

Prince Andrew starts a new job as a Royal Navy Helicopter Pilot on board HMS Brazen, Plymouth, June, 1984

Getty Images

AB InBev

Our dream is to be the Best Beer Company in a Better World

Everyone at AB InBev UK would like to congratulate Her Majesty the Queen on her Diamond Jubilee. Her Majesty's role as a leader and as head of state, plus her lifetime's service to others is truly an inspiration. This is a very special occasion and every member of our staff wishes Her Majesty all the best for her sixty years on the throne and many more to come. Cheers to you Ma'am!

About AB InBev UK Ltd

AB InBev UK makes many of the UK's best-loved drinks – from our oldest trademark Bass, to our most recent Stella Artois Cidre.

We employ around 1,400 people at our UK breweries at Magor, Samlesbury and in Mortlake – as well as at our company headquarters in Luton.

Beer is a drink for togetherness and celebration at home or in that most British institution – the pub. What better way for people to enjoy this very special occasion. We hope you will join us in raising a glass to Her Majesty.

Best Beer Company in a Better World

We are proud of our heritage here in the UK – and of our efforts to be the Best Beer Company in a Better World.

Anheuser-Busch InBev is the beer industry leader in social responsibility initiatives. Our efforts focus on three pillars: promoting responsible drinking; protecting the environment; and giving back to the communities in which we live and work.

To find out more about us visit: www.ab-inbev.co.uk

drinkaware.co.uk for the facts

Please drink responsibly

Charles, Prince of Wales

RANK: Captain, Pilot;

BRANCH OF SERVICE: RAF, RN;

UNIT: 845 Naval Air Squadron;

YEARS OF SERVICE: 1971–1976;

MILITARY TRAINING: Royal Naval College Dartmouth.

Following in the tradition of the Princes of Wales before him, Prince Charles spent time in the navy and air force. During his second year at Cambridge, he went to the Royal Air Force College Cranwell to train as a jet pilot. After the passing out parade in September of that year, he embarked on a naval career, enrolling in a course at the Royal Naval College Dartmouth and then serving on the guided missile destroyer HMS Norfolk (1971–72) the HMS Minerva (1972–73) and HMS Jupiter (1974).

He also qualified as a helicopter pilot at RNAS Yeovilton prior to joining 845 Naval Air Squadron in 1974. In 1976, Prince Charles took command of the coastal minehunter HMS Bronington for his last nine months in the navy.

Prince Edward, Earl of Wessex

RANK: Acting Lieutenant;

BRANCH OF SERVICE: Royal Marines;

YEARS OF SERVICE: 1986–1987;

MILITARY TRAINING: Commando Training Centre Royal Marines.

On leaving university, Prince Edward joined the Royal Marines to train as an officer cadet. However, he resigned his commission in January 1987, before completing training. He became more involved in theatre, and went on to set up his own production company. The Earl carries out a number of Royal duties on behalf of the Queen, and has taken on many roles from his father, the Duke of Edinburgh.

"The Duke of Kent was promoted to Major-General in 1983 and to Field Marshal 10 years later"

Prince Michael of Kent

RANK: Major;

BRANCH OF SERVICE: British Army;

WAR SERVICE: Cyprus, Germany, Hong Kong;

UNIT: 11th Hussars;

YEARS OF SERVICE: 1963–1981;

MILITARY TRAINING: Royal Military Academy Sandhurst.

Prince Michael entered the Royal Military Academy Sandhurst in 1961, where he was commissioned into the 11th Hussars. He served in Germany, Hong Kong, and Cyprus, where his squadron formed part of the UN peacekeeping force of 1971. Subsequent tours of duty – during a military career that spanned 20 years – included a number of appointments on the Defence Intelligence Staff. In 1981, he retired from the army with the rank of Major.

In 1994, he was made Honorary Rear Admiral of the Royal Naval Reserve, and in 2002, he was made Honorary Air Commodore of RAF Benson. In 2009, he was appointed Honorary Regimental Colonel of the Honourable Artillery Company, and he is colonel-in-chief of the Essex and Kent Scottish Regiment in Canada.

Prince Edward, Duke of Kent

RANK: Lieutenant-Colonel;

BRANCH OF SERVICE: British Army;

WAR SERVICE: Cyprus and Hong Kong;

UNIT: Royal Scots Greys;

YEARS OF SERVICE: 1955-1976;

MILITARY TRAINING: Royal Military Academy Sandhurst.

In a military career that spanned more than 20 years, the Duke of Kent graduated from the Royal Military Academy Sandhurst in 1955 as a Second Lieutenant in the Royal Scots Greys. He was promoted to captain in 1961 and served in Hong Kong from 1962–63. He was promoted to Major in 1967, and in 1970 he served in the British Sovereign base area in Cyprus; part of the UN peacekeeping force between the Greek and Turkish parts of the island. He was promoted to Lieutenant-Colonel in 1973 and three years later retired from the army. He was subsequently promoted to Major-General in 1983 and to Field Marshal 10 years later.

>>

From left: Prince Edward at RAF Benson, April, 1984. Charles, Prince of Wales, during a visit to RAF Wittering, July, 1977. Prince Michael of Kent marching in a parade at Sandhurst, December 1961. Prince Edward, Duke of Kent, at a Trooping of the Colour ceremony in London, June 1978

Getty Images

IL SOGNO
THE DREAM

We at Il Sogno are delighted to offer Her Majesty our sincere congratulations on the celebration of her Diamond jubilee; she is an inspiration to us all.
Long may she reign!

Il Sogno is situated on the borders of Umbria and Tuscany, presenting the best of Italian countryside, culture and cuisine.

Recommended by *JetSetter* magazine, we have now decided to open our doors for a limited period each year to share our unique family home.

The 17th century building has been lovingly restored and offers an atmosphere that personifies this region; with rolling vineyards, olive groves and fruit trees, covering the three acre estate.

The interior is designed to be luxurious and subtle, allowing you to take in the ambience and idyllic environment in perfect comfort; enjoying fine wine and food, all prepared on site.

We also have a fully-equipped spa, gym and full sized tennis court for you to really work up an appetite for the delights available. With extensive staff and a personal butler on hand, we ensure that our guests receive a six star royal experience they will never forget.

www.il-sogno-italy.com - We welcome you to share our dream
For reservations emai kikiss@gmail.com or call tel number : 39-07596-59020
- U.K - 0800-066-4722 U.S.A - 1-877-573-8872

> "The Queen was the first female member of the Royal Family to become a full-time active member of the services"

Prince Philip, Duke of Edinburgh

RANK: Lieutenant;

BRANCH OF SERVICE: Royal Navy;

WAR SERVICE: World War II, Allied invasion of Sicily, Battle of Crete, Battle of Cape Matapan;

UNIT: British Pacific Fleet;

YEARS OF SERVICE: 1940-unknown;

MILITARY TRAINING: Royal Naval College Greenwich;

MEDALS: War Medal 1939-1945, Atlantic Star, Africa Star, Burma Star, Italy Star, Greek War Cross, Croix de Guerre 1939-1945.

Prince Philip joined the Royal Navy in 1939, graduating the following year from Dartmouth as the top cadet in his year.

He spent four months on the battleship HMS Ramillies, protecting convoys of the Australian Expeditionary Force in the Indian Ocean, followed by shorter postings in Ceylon (now Sri Lanka). After the invasion of Greece by Italy in 1940, he was transferred from the Indian Ocean to the battleship HMS Valiant in the Mediterranean fleet. He served in the Battle of Crete and the Battle of Cape Matapan and was awarded the Greek War Cross of Valour for his service.

At just 21 years of age, he became First Lieutenant of HMS Wallace – one of the youngest first Lieutenants in the Royal Navy. During the invasion of Sicily in 1943, he saved his ship from a night bomb attack and he was present in Tokyo Bay when Japanese surrender was signed.

Queen Elizabeth II

RANK: Subaltern;

BRANCH OF SERVICE: Auxiliary Territorial Service, British Army War Service: World War II;

YEARS OF SERVICE: 1945–1949;

MEDALS: War Medal 1939-1945, Defence Medal.

As Princess Elizabeth, in 1945, Her Majesty The Queen joined the Auxillary Territorial Service as Second Subaltern, a rank equivalent to Second Lieutenant. She was the first female member of the Royal Family to become a full-time active member of the services. By the end of World War II, the heiress to the British throne had risen through the military ranks to become a Junior Commander and a fully qualified driver. In 1947, Princess Elizabeth made her first official overseas visit to South Africa and on her 21st birthday, she made a broadcast to the British Empire pledging her dedication to the people of the Commonwealth.

Princess Elizabeth, as then was, driving an ambulance during her wartime service in the Auxiliary Territorial Service, April 1945 (above left). Prince Philip in his Royal Navy uniform (above)

Getty Images

>>

"Lord Mountbatten was responsible for overseeing the transition of British India to independence in 1947"

Lord Mountbatten, 1st Earl of Mountbatten of Burma, Commander of the Mediterranean Fleet, on naval exercises in Malta and Gibralta in 1956 (above)

Lord Mountbatten, 1st Earl, Mountbatten of Burma

RANK: Admiral of the Fleet;

BRANCH OF SERVICE: Royal Navy;

WAR SERVICE: World War I and World War II;

UNIT: 5th Destroyer Flotilla;

YEARS OF SERVICE: 1914-1945;

MILITARY TRAINING: Naval Cadet School;

MEDALS: Order of Merit, Distinguished Service Order.

Lord Mountbatten served in the Royal Navy as a midshipman during World War I and when World War II broke out in 1939, he was moved to active service as commander of the 5th Destroyer Flotilla on board the HMS Kelly. He led a British convoy in a mission to evacuate the Allied Forces involved in the Namsos campaign. He played a significant role planning the raid at St Nazaire – an operation resulting in disuse of one of the most heavily defended docks in Nazi-occupied France. He was

involved in the ill-fated Dieppe Raid of 1942 and argued that the lessons learned from that were necessary for planning the Normandy invasion on D-Day nearly two years later.

In October 1943, Winston Churchill appointed Lord Mountbatten the Supreme Allied Commander South East Asia Command, and during this time, he oversaw the recapture of Burma from the Japanese.

He was responsible for overseeing the transition of British India to independence in 1947 and for this he was appointed Viceroy of India. Resigned to the fact that a united India was unlikely, he arranged for partition, creating the independent nations of India and Pakistan.

He returned to the Mediterranean to serve as Commander-in-Chief and served his final posting as First Sea Lord until 1959.

Getty Images

>>

The CW Publishing Group...
delivering results for our contract partners

You & Your Family – free magazine for pregnant women, in association with RCOG

Baby & You – free magazine for new mums, in association with MIDIRS

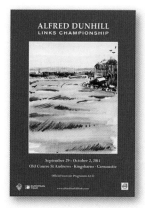

Alfred Dunhill Links Championship Official Souvenir Programme – for the Richemont Group

Exchanged – free magazine for new homeowners, in association with NAEA

"We find the hardest things in publishing the easiest things to do"

BRING YOUR COMPANY TO LIFE WITH CW PUBLISHING

LONDON • NEW YORK
cwpublishinggroup

Congratulations

3663 are delighted to offer Her Majesty Queen Elizabeth our sincere congratulations on this auspicious royal occasion.

As royal warrant holders, 3663 have provided many years of service to the royal households. 3663 take much pleasure in supporting the 'great' in Britain by ensuring quality traditional British produce is available to all our customers, including produce from local and regional suppliers.

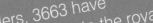

3663
inspired **by you**

"George VI played an important role during the Battle of Jutland in WWI – an attack against the German Navy"

King George VI

RANK: Commander;
BRANCH OF SERVICE: Royal Navy and Royal Air Force;
WAR SERVICE: World War I;
UNIT: HMS Collingwood Royal Naval Air Service and RAF Cranwell;
YEARS OF SERVICE: 1909–1918;
MILITARY TRAINING: Britannia Royal Naval College.

King George VI was the first member of the Royal Family to be certified as a fully qualified pilot. From 1909, he attended the Royal Naval College Osborne as a naval cadet, progressing to the Royal Naval College Dartmouth. He trained on the HMS Cumberland in the West Indies and on the east coast of Canada. As a midshipman aboard the HMS Collingwood, he spent three months in the Mediterranean before beginning service in World War I. He played an important role during the Battle of Jutland —an attack against the German Navy that was considered the largest naval action of the war.

Due to ill health, he did not serve in a war again but was appointed Officer in Charge at the Royal Naval Air Service's training establishment at Cranwell. With the establishment of the Royal Air Force and the transfer of Cranwell from Navy to Air Force control, he transferred from the Royal Navy to the Royal Air Force and was appointed Officer Commanding at Cranwell where he remained until 1918.

Edward VIII, Duke of Windsor

RANK: Lieutenant;
BRANCH OF SERVICE: British Army, Royal Air Force;
WAR SERVICE: World War I;
UNIT: Grenadier Guards;
YEARS OF SERVICE: 1914-1918;
MEDALS: Military Cross.

When World War I broke out, Edward had reached the minimum age for active service and joined the Grenadier Guards in 1914. He was willing to serve on the frontline but the Secretary of State for War refused. However, despite this, Edward often visited the frontline and for this he was awarded the Military Cross in 1916. His role in the war, although limited, made him popular among veterans. He undertook his first military flight in 1918 and later gained his pilot's licence.

After his abdication, he was created Duke of Windsor and later during World War II, he was at first stationed with the British Military Mission to France and later dispatched to the Bahamas after his appointment as Governor. He spent the remainder of his life in retirement in France. ◼

George VI as a midshipman in the Royal Navy during World War I, circa 1914 (above left). Edward Albert Windsor, Prince of Wales, as Second Lieutenant in the Grenadier Guards, 1914 (above right)

Getty Images

Celebrations for the Diamond Jubilee of Her Majesty The Queen

It is an immense honour and privilege to take part in the celebrations marking the Diamond Jubilee of Her Majesty The Queen. Only one other British Monarch has achieved this milestone – Queen Victoria – who continues to be the name of our beautiful harbour. Like her predecessor, Her Majesty has presided the British Empire and the Commonwealth for 60 years stretching from the shores of the Falkland Islands to Gibraltar, and all the way to New Zealand.

Her Majesty The Queen made her first visit to Hong Kong in 1975, and visited again in 1986 after she became the first British Monarch to set foot in the People's Republic of China. This came only a couple of years after it was agreed that Hong Kong would return to Chinese rule in 1997.

We don't have to dig very deep to find the ties between our city and the United Kingdom such as its rule of law, its institutions, its legislative system, and the English language.

Hong Kong has become such a beacon of success in China and beyond precisely because we have managed to mix our unique Chinese and British heritage, bringing together the very best of east and west. The United Kingdom established well-respected and independent institutions, laying a strong foundation for Hong Kong's future. We have since returned to China, embraced its vibrant economy, and capitalized on its many opportunities. This has turned Hong Kong into one of the leading cities of the world.

Hong Kong would not be the globally-recognized city we are today without its thriving financial markets. It was under British rule, back in 1865, when the first seeds of today's spectacular success were planted. England passed the Companies Act in 1862, and then introduced a similar piece of legislation in Hong Kong called the Companies Ordinance in 1865. However, it wasn't until the Association of Stock Brokers was formed in 1891 that trading began at a fixed location during fixed hours. This marked the birth of the Hong Kong Stock Exchange, which has since grown into one of the world's most dynamic and successful exchange. The key factors include our rule of law, a highly respected and independent judiciary, international best practices and standards, a highly professional and skilled workforce and free flow of capital and information. Indeed, for the past ten years, Hong Kong Exchanges and Clearing ("HKEx") has been one of the top five IPO fund-raising exchanges, a distinction shared only by the NYSE-Euronext Exchange. For 2011, HKEx also topped the global IPO funds raised table for the third consecutive year and was named the world's leading financial market by the World Economic Forum.

When the Union Jack was lowered in 1997, Britain left behind a strong legacy: one of the world's freest economies, world class infrastructure, a lively and free press, political stability, the rule of law, and a clean and open government. We have further excelled in all of these areas in the years since reunification with China. This is a tremendous accomplishment for Hong Kong, and has driven our city's success over the past several decades.

It is with great pride that I extend to Her Majesty The Queen HKEx's heartiest congratulations on her Diamond Jubilee, and long may she reign.

The Hon. Ronald Arculli, GBM, CVO, GBS, OBE, JP

Hong Kong Exchanges and Clearing Limited

12/F, One International Finance Centre, 1 Harbour View Street, Central, Hong Kong

Tel   +852 2522 1122
Fax   +852 2295 3106
Website www.hkex.com.hk
Email   info@hkex.com.hk

THE ROYAL BRITISH LEGION

Celebrating our Patron's Diamond Jubilee

Providing help, advice and support to serving members of the Armed Forces, ex-Service men and women and their families.

To donate to our work call **020 3207 2275** or visit **www.britishlegion.org.uk**

Shoulder to shoulder with all who Serve

Reg. Charity No. 219279

The Victorian Jubilee

Queen Elizabeth II is not the only monarch to have celebrated 60 years. Over 100 years ago Queen Victoria reached her Diamond Jubilee year. We look at how the country and the world celebrated the big day

This summer the country will be awash with Union flags, smiling faces and cheer: A typically British celebration of its monarchy, last seen at the Royal Wedding in April 2011. At times of National celebration, the British stiff upper lip and stoicism is cast aside and communities join together and rejoice in their homes and streets. But is this a new occurrence? Certainly not. The street parties of today hark back to the street parties of yesteryear: VE day, Prince Charles and Diana Spencer's wedding and the Queen's Golden Jubilee have all seen huge outpourings of public jubilance.

A glittering affair

Nearly 120 years ago, on the 22 June 1897, it was the turn of another great British Queen to celebrate her Diamond Jubilee: Queen Victoria, our longest serving monarch >>

Queen Victoria (1819-1901) on the occasion of her Diamond Jubilee, after a reign of 60 years, 1897 (above)

Getty Images

"The only way to watch the festivities was to head to London and so thousands of people flocked there to see the procession"

Well wishers balance on the roof of Buckingham Palace as the State coach passes into the courtyard during the Diamond Jubilee, 1897

at 63 years and seven months, and still the longest serving female monarch ever. At 78 years old, Queen Victoria had initially hoped for a quiet commemoration after her huge Golden Jubilee, 10 years previously; however it became clear that her people wanted her to celebrate with a glittering affair. It was suggested that the Diamond Jubilee become a celebration of the British Empire, which the Queen agreed to. So, though frail, the Queen presided over an impressive calendar of events that are remembered in history.

Empress of India

The accession anniversary of 20 June 1897 fell on a Sunday and was marked with special services around the country,

with the Queen attending St George's Chapel, Windsor. Troops from across the Empire paraded through the streets in her honour. Victoria, also Empress of India, entered the thanksgiving service on the arm of an Indian servant and the following day, she returned to London to receive foreign envoys to enjoy the Torchlight Military Tattoo in the grounds of Buckingham Palace.

"My beloved people"

The official celebration of the Diamond Jubilee took place on Tuesday, 22 June 1897. In the morning, the Queen transmitted a telegram to the world with the personal message: "From my heart I thank my beloved people. May God bless them." The only way to watch the >>

MICROLINK
Universal Inclusivity

Your Majesty the Queen

On behalf of myself and my colleagues at Microlink PC UK Ltd, I am extremely proud and honoured to contribute my warmest congratulations alongside those included within The Royal British Legion Queen's Diamond Jubilee celebration.

As an organisation operating in an industry providing professional services for people with disabilities over the past 20 years, we have witnessed and experienced the extraordinary progress British society has made towards an industry which has traditionally suffered from significant stigmas. Your Majesty's active presence has encouraged an awareness to the nation that disability is not inability and that our society is one of inclusivity. Our nation is now synonymous with its developed sense of practical empathy, which shows a level of maturity that we have secured in both social and legal frameworks.

Glimpsing at "yesterday" to arrive at "today", within your 60 years Your Majesty has given Royal Assents to some 3,500 Acts of Parliament, been on 261 official overseas visits, hosted 96 state visits, seen 12 different Prime Ministers, given patronage to over 600 charities/organisations and held 610 Investitures to name a few of your royal duties.

I am honoured to have this opportunity to pay tribute to Your Majesty, who has given such splendid service to our country, making it the leading beacon of light in the world. I wish Your Majesty continued good health and happiness.

Dr Nasser Siabi OBE

www.microlinkpc.com
Microlink PC (UK) Ltd, Microlink House, Brickfield Lane, Chandlers Ford, Hampshire SO53 4DP
Freephone 0800 999 2620 Fax 023 8024 0310

Brompton Bicycle Ltd has been manufacturing its bicycles in West London for over a quarter of a century. We remain committed to excellence in design and engineering, to making useful products that delight and last, and to manufacturing in the UK.

What we have achieved, and what we aspire to in the future, owes much to the support of Her Majesty the Queen.

In 1995, the Queen's Award for Export Achievement brought a small manufacturer to the attention of a much broader public and set us on course to becoming the UK's largest bicycle manufacturer.

In 2010, the Queen's Awards for Enterprise in both Innovation and Export Achievement again helped Brompton to distinguish itself from its competitors, particularly in its export markets, which now account for 75% of its sales.

On behalf of ourselves and the thousands of British businesses that have benefitted from Her Majesty's patronage, we congratulate The Queen on 60 glorious years, and wish Her many happy returns.

BROMPTON

personal transport

Getty Images

Crowds line the streets to watch Queen Victoria pass in her Diamond Jubilee procession

festivities before television was to head to London and so thousands of people flocked to catch a glimpse of the Royal procession. Sailors in boaters pulled gun carriages on ropes while guards in bearskin hats and tunics lined the roads. Among many others, the Indian Lancers in their turbans, the Jamaican Artillery and New Zealand Mounted Troops had travelled to take part in the parade, joined by the traditional Sovereign's Escort of the 2nd Life Guards.

Victoria, dressed in black silk with a black bonnet decorated with white ostrich feathers and diamonds, proceeded through London in a carriage to St Paul's Cathedral for a service, across London Bridge, through south London and back past Parliament to Buckingham Palace. The Queen looked resplendent in a carriage pulled by eight, cream regal horses accompanied by Helena, Princess Christian of Schleswig-Holstein

>>

"For the festivities, the Princess of Wales initiated a project to hold the biggest banquet in the world to feed London's poor"

The year after the Diamond Jubilee, 1898, an elderly Queen Victoria is surrounded by the royal family at Osborne House, including her successor Edward VII

(third daughter of Queen Victoria) and The Princess of Wales (later Queen Alexandra).

Deeply touching

Victoria wrote emotionally in her journal that night: "No-one ever, I believe, has met with such an ovation as was given to me, passing through those six miles of streets... The crowds were quite indescribable and their enthusiasm truly marvellous and deeply touching. "The cheering was quite deafening and every face seemed to be filled with real joy."

As the Queen walked with difficulty and was unable to climb the steps to the Cathedral, it was decided to hold the morning service outside with Queen Victoria remaining in her carriage. A 'Te Deum' (a hymn of praise) was sung on the steps of the Cathedral overseen by The Warders of the Tower of London who were stationed on the steps of St Paul's Cathedral during the thanksgiving service in front of a huge crowd of well wishers.

There was one mishap during the procession when the elderly Gold Stick, Lord Howe – tasked with protecting the sovereign – fainted, although he did remount to be greeted by cheers from the crowd, according to Debrett's look back at the commemoration. Instead, The Archbishop of Canterbury embarked on a spontaneous three cheers for the Queen.

A grand dinner

In the evening on the official Jubilee Day, there was a grand dinner party at Buckingham Palace where the Queen's table was decorated with a 9ft high display of 60,000 orchids from every part of the then Empire, crafted into the shape of a crown. There were also royal engagements all week long, including a State Ball at the Palace and a mass Naval review at Spithead in Hampshire attended by the then Prince of Wales and involving 165 ships. Jubilee hymns were commissioned and society garden parties hosted by various Countesses; while a reception and ball was held by the Corporation of the City of London at the Guildhall.

As part of the festivities, Alexandra, Princess of Wales, initiated a project to hold the biggest banquet in the world and feed 400,000 of London's poor. She staged a series of vast Diamond Jubilee Feasts where everyone was welcome no matter what their background or what state their clothes were in. More than 700 tons of food was needed and 10,000 waiters with the meals backed by millionaire Sir Thomas Lipton. Diners ate roast ribs of beef and veal and ham pies, followed by dates, oranges and a drink of English ale or ginger beer and then pipes and tobacco. Queen Victoria died just three and a half years later in January 1901 at the age of 81 and was succeeded by Edward VII. She left behind a large family, including her nine children. ∎

Getty Images

Did you know?

A fact for every year of Her Majesty the Queen's reign.

The Queen and the Duke of Edinburgh attend a service for The Order of The British Emplire at St Paul's Cathedral, London, 2012 (above)

1 The Queen is the second longest serving monarch after Queen Victoria, who reigned for 63 years. Only five other kings and queens in British history have reigned for 50 years or more. All of them younger than Queen Elizabeth II at their Golden Jubilees. They are:
- Victoria (63 years);
- George III (59 years);
- Henry III (56 years);
- Edward III (50 years);
- James VI of Scotland (James I of England) (58 years).

2 Since 1952 the Queen has given Royal Assent to more than 3500 Acts of Parliament.

3. Her Majesty has had 12 prime ministers:
- Sir Winston Churchill 1951-55;
- Sir Anthony Eden 1955-57;
- Harold Macmillan 1957-63;
- Sir Alec Douglas-Home 1963-64;
- Harold Wilson 1964-70 and 1974-76;
- Sir Edward Heath 1970-74;
- James Callaghan 1976-79;
- Margaret Thatcher 1979-90;
- John Major 1990-97;
- Tony Blair 1997-2007;
- Gordon Brown 2007-2010;
- David Cameron 2010 – present.

8 There have been six Archbishops of Canterbury, soon to be seven, during the Queen's reign (Archbishops Geoffrey Fisher, Michael Ramsey, Donald Coggan, Robert Runcie, George Carey and recently-retired Rowan Williams).

9 There have been six Roman Catholic Popes during the Queen's reign (Pius XII, John XXIII, Paul VI, John Paul I, John Paul II, Benedict XVI).

10 Many of the Queen's official tours were undertaken on the Royal Yacht Britannia. It was launched by Her Majesty on 16 April 1953 and was commissioned for service on 7 January 1954. It was de-commissioned in December 1997. During this time, Britannia travelled more than a million miles on royal and official duties.

11 The Queen is the 40th monarch since William the Conqueror obtained the crown of England.

12 The Queen has received two Popes on visits to the UK (Pope John Paul II in 1982 and Pope Benedict XVI in 2010). Pope John Paul II's visit in 1982 was the first Papal visit to the United Kingdom for over 450 years. The Queen has officially visited the Vatican twice in her reign – in 1961 visiting Pope John XXIII and in 1980 visiting Pope John Paul II.

13 The Queen is currently patron of over 600 charities and organisations, over 400 of which she has held since 1952.   >>

4 The Royal Yacht Britannia was first used by the Queen when Her Majesty embarked with the Duke of Edinburgh on 1 May 1954 at Tobruk for the final stage of their Commonwealth Tour returning to the Pool of London. The last time The Queen was on board Britannia for an official visit was on the 9 August 1997 for a visit to Arran in Scotland.

Queen Elizabeth II, accompanied by Prince Philip, waves to the crowd as she leaves for the Opening of Parliament, 2000 (above). Deckhands meet for a reunion onboard the Royal Yacht Britannia, 2009 (right)

5 Tony Blair was the first Prime Minister to have been born during the Queen's reign. He was born in early May, 1953 – a month before the Coronation.

6 The Queen's racing colours are a purple body with gold braid, scarlet sleeves and black velvet cap with gold fringe. They were adopted from those used by King Edward VII; one of his most successful horses was called Diamond Jubilee.

7 The Queen has attended every opening of Parliament except those in 1959 and 1963, when she was expecting Prince Andrew and Prince Edward respectively.

Getty Images

14 Since 1952, The Queen has conferred over 404,500 honours and awards.

15 The Queen has personally held over 610 Investitures.

16 The first Investiture of the Queen's reign took place at Buckingham Palace on 27 February 1952. The first person to be presented was Private William Speakman, of The King's Own Scottish Borderers, who received the Victoria Cross for his actions during the Korean War.

17 Since it was launched to mark the Queen's Golden Jubilee in 2002, The Queen's Award for Voluntary Service has been awarded to over 750 voluntary organisations across all four countries in the UK. Winners of the award have included local scout groups, community radio stations, groups that care for the elderly and environmental charities.

18 The Queen has answered around three and a half million items of correspondence.

19 The Queen has sent almost 540,000 telegrams to couples in the UK and the Commonwealth celebrating their diamond wedding (60 years) anniversary.

20 The Queen and the Duke of Edinburgh have sent approximately 45,000 Christmas cards during the Queen's reign.

21 In 60 years, the Queen has undertaken 261 official overseas visits, including 96 State Visits to 116 different countries.

22 In 60 years, The Queen has often travelled to her major Realms. Her Majesty has visited Australia 18 times, Canada 22 times, Jamaica six times and New Zealand 10 times.

23 The Queen's official visits have ranged from the Cocos Islands, 5.4 square miles with a population of 596, to the People's Republic of China, 3.7 million square miles with a population of 1.34 billion.

24 The Queen made an historic visit to the Republic of Ireland in May 2011, the first visit by a British

Queen Elizabeth II is given flowers by children in Ottawa, Canada, 2010 (above). The trip was to celebrate the centenary of the Canadian Navy and to mark Canada Day on 6 July

Monarch since Irish independence (King George V visited in 1911).

25 Unusual live gifts given to the Queen on foreign tours include: two tortoises given to the Queen in the Seychelles in 1972; a seven-year-old bull elephant called Jumbo given to Her Majesty by the President of Cameroon in 1972 to mark the Queen's Silver Wedding, and two black beavers given to the Queen after a royal visit to Canada.

26 The only time the Queen has had to interrupt an overseas tour was in 1974 during a tour of Australia and Indonesia. The Queen was called back to the UK from Australia when a general election in the UK was suddenly called. The Duke of Edinburgh continued the programme in Australia, and the Queen rejoined the tour in Indonesia.

27 The Queen has given out approximately 90,000 Christmas puddings to staff continuing the custom of King George V and King George VI.

28 Her Majesty's first Commonwealth tour, as Queen, began on 24 November 1953, and included visits to Canada, Bermuda, Jamaica, Panama, Fiji, Tonga, New Zealand, Australia, the Cocos Islands, Ceylon, Aden, Uganda,

Queen Elizabeth II watches a Chinese Lion dance troop perform during her visit to the Toa Payoh Housing Development in Singapore, 2006

Getty Images

Libya, Malta and Gibraltar. The total distance covered was 43,618 miles.

29 The Queen has sent over 175,000 telegrams to centenarians in the UK and the Commonwealth.

30 There have been 102 inward State Visits from 1952 to the end of 2011 (up to and including Turkey in November 2011).

31 The Queen and The Duke of Edinburgh have been married for 64 years. They were married on 20 November 1947 in Westminster Abbey. The Queen's wedding dress was designed by Norman Hartnell and was woven at Winterthur Silks Limited, Dunfermline, in the Canmore factory, using silk that had come from Chinese silkworms at Lullingstone Castle.

32 The first football match the Queen attended was the 1953 FA Cup Final.

33 The Queen has laid her wreath at the Cenotaph on Remembrance Sunday every year of her reign, except in 1959, 1961, 1963, 1968, 1983 and 1999.

34 The Queen has attended 56 Royal Maundy services in 43 Cathedrals during her reign. A total of 6710 people have received Maundy Money in recognition of their service to the Church and their communities.

35 The Queen has attended 35 Royal Variety performances.

36 The Queen has launched 21 ships during her reign.

37 Over the course of her reign, almost one and a half million people have attended garden parties at Buckingham Palace or the Palace of Holyroodhouse (The Queen ended Debutante Presentation Parties in 1958).

38 During the Silver Jubilee year, the Queen toured 36 counties in the UK and Northern Ireland, starting in Glasgow on the 17 May. During her Golden Jubilee year the Queen toured 35 counties, beginning in Cornwall on 1 May.

39 In 1969 the first television film about the family life of the Royal Family was made, and shown on the eve of the Investiture of Prince Charles as Prince of Wales. >>

40 The Queen has sat for 129 portraits during her reign.

41 An important innovation during the Queen's reign was the opening in 1962 of a new gallery at Buckingham Palace to display items from the Royal Collection. The brainchild of the Duke of Edinburgh, the new Queen's Gallery occupied the space of the Palace's bomb-damaged private chapel. It was the first time that parts of the Palace had been opened to the general public. The new Queen's Gallery was redeveloped and re-opened in 2002 for the Golden Jubilee.

42 The Queen launched the British Monarchy's official website in 1997. In 2007 the official British Monarchy YouTube channel was unveiled, swiftly followed by a Royal Twitter site (2009), Flickr page (2010) and Facebook page (also 2010).

43 The Queen has made a Christmas Broadcast to the Commonwealth every year of her reign except 1969, when a repeat of the film *Royal Family* was shown and a written message from the Queen issued. In 2002 the Queen made her 50th Christmas Broadcast and in 2004 the Queen issued her first separate broadcast for members of the British Armed Forces.

44 In 1953, the Queen made the first Christmas Broadcast from overseas, (rather than from the UK), broadcasting live from New Zealand. The first televised broadcast was in 1957, made live. The first pre-recorded broadcast took place in 1960 to allow transmission around the world. In 2006 the Christmas Broadcast was first made available to download as a podcast.

45 The Queen hosts "theme days" and receptions to promote and celebrate aspects of British culture. Recent examples from 2011 include a reception for Young People and the Performing Arts and for Explorers. Other themes have included Publishing, Broadcasting, Tourism, Emergency Services, Maritime Day, Music, Young Achievers, British Design, and Pioneers.

46 In an average year, the Queen will host more than 50,000 people at banquets, lunches, dinners, receptions and garden parties at Buckingham Palace. The Queen also hosts more than 8000 people each year at garden parties and investitures at Holyroodhouse,

A member of the Household Cavalry, wearing traditional ceremonial uniform, bearing the royal insignia of Queen Elizabeth II, at Trooping the Colour, London, 2007 (above). Queen Elizabeth II hosts a garden party, June, 2010 (right)

during Holyrood Week. To be invited to a garden party at Buckingham palace is a very exciting and priviledged event the world over.

47 The first Royal Walkabout took place during the visit by the Queen and the Duke of Edinburgh to Australia and New Zealand in 1970. The practice was introduced to allow them to meet as many people as possible, not simply officials and dignitaries.

48 The Queen was born at 17 Bruton St, London W1 on the 21 April 1926, was christened on the 29 May 1926 in the Private Chapel at Buckingham Palace and was confirmed on the 28 March 1942 in the Private Chapel at Windsor Castle.

49 The Queen learnt to drive in 1945. She has been seen driving herself around Windsor Great Park on her way to Windsor Castle.

50 With the birth of Prince Andrew in 1960, the Queen became the first reigning sovereign to have a child since Queen Victoria, who had her youngest child, Princess Beatrice, in 1857. She then, of course, went on to have more children during her reign.

51 The Queen's real birthday is on 21 April, but it is celebrated officially in June.

52 The Queen's first foreign tour of the Silver Jubilee year was a visit to Western Samoa, Tonga, Fiji, New Zealand, Australia and Papua New Guinea. The first foreign tour of the Queen's Golden Jubilee year was to Jamaica, New Zealand and Australia.

53 The Queen has 30 godchildren.

54 The Queen has owned more than 30 corgis during her reign, starting with Susan who was a present for her 18th birthday in 1944. A good proportion of these have been direct descendants from Susan. Her Majesty currently has three corgis – Monty, Willow and Holly.

55 The Queen also introduced a new breed of dog known as the "dorgi" when one of Her Majesty's corgis was mated with a dachshund named Pipkin which belonged to Princess Margaret. There have been 11 dorgis including Tinker, Pickles, Chipper, Piper, Harris, Brandy, Berry, Cider and Vulcan.

56 The Queen's wedding ring was made from a nugget of Welsh gold, which came from the Clogau St David's mine near Dolgellau. The official wedding cake was made by McVitie and Price Ltd.

57 The wedding of the Queen and the Duke of Edinburgh was the first and so far the only time in British history that the heir presumptive to the throne had been married.

58 The Queen has been at the saluting base of her troops in every Trooping the Colour ceremony since the start of her reign, with the exception of 1955, when a national rail strike forced the cancellation of the parade.

59 Queen Victoria was the last and to date the only British Monarch to celebrate a Diamond Jubilee. The Queen, who will be aged 85 on Accession Day in 2012, will be the oldest monarch to celebrate a Diamond Jubilee.

60 There have been only three Diamond Jubilees of Heads of State celebrated throughout the world during the Queen's reign. King Bhumibol Adulyadej of Thailand; the former Sultan of Johor (now a part of Malaysia) and the late Emperor Hirohito of Japan.

Advertisers' Index